W9-BEE-229

Southern China, Hong Kong, and Taiwan

Significant Issues Series

SIGNIFICANT ISSUES SERIES papers are written for and published by the Center for Strategic and International Studies.

Series Editors:	David M. Abshire
	Douglas M. Johnston
Director of Studies:	Erik R. Peterson
Director of Publications:	Nancy B. Eddy
Managing Editor:	Roberta L. Howard
Associate Editors:	Donna R. Spitler
	Yoma Ullman
Editorial Assistant:	Kathleen M. McTigue

The Center for Strategic and International Studies (CSIS), established in 1962, is a private, tax-exempt institution focusing on international public policy issues. Its research is nonpartisan and nonproprietary.

CSIS is dedicated to policy analysis and impact. It seeks to inform and shape selected policy decisions in government and the private sector to meet the increasingly complex and difficult global challenges that leaders will confront in the next century. It achieves this mission in three ways: by generating strategic analysis that is anticipatory and interdisciplinary; by convening policymakers and other influential parties to assess key issues; and by building structures for policy action.

CSIS does not take specific public policy positions. Accordingly, all views, positions, and conclusions expressed in this publication should be understood to be solely those of the authors.

❖   ❖   ❖

Based in Honolulu, the **Pacific Forum CSIS** operates as the autonomous Asia-Pacific arm of CSIS. Founded in 1975, the thrust of the Forum's work is to help develop cooperative policies in the Asia-Pacific region through debate and analyses undertaken with the region's leaders in the academic, government, and corporate arenas. The Forum collaborates with a network of more than 30 research institutes around the Pacific Rim, drawing on Asian perspectives and disseminating its projects' findings and recommendations to opinion leaders, governments, and publics throughout the region.

The Center for Strategic and International Studies
1800 K Street, N.W.
Washington, D.C.   20006
Telephone: (202) 887-0200
Fax: (202) 775-3199

Southern China, Hong Kong, and Taiwan
Evolution of a Subregional Economy

Edited by *Jane Khanna*

Foreword by *Robert A. Scalapino*

THE CENTER FOR STRATEGIC & INTERNATIONAL STUDIES
Washington, D.C.

HC
427.92
S634
1995

Cover design by Meadows Design Office.

Significant Issues Series, Volume XVII, Number 7
© 1995 by The Center for Strategic and International Studies
Washington, D.C. 20006
Printed on recycled paper in the United States of America

99 98 97 96 95   5 4 3 2 1

ISSN 0736-7136
ISBN 0-89206-321-1

Library of Congress Cataloging-in-Publication Data

Southern China, Hong Kong, and Taiwan : evolution of a
   subregional economy / editor, Jane Khanna.
      p. cm. -- (Significant issues series, ISSN 0736-7136 ;
   v. 17, no. 7)
   Includes bibliographical references.
   ISBN 0-89206-321-1
      1. China, Southeast—Economic conditions.   2. Hong Kong—
   Economic conditions.   3. Taiwan—Economic conditions—1975–
   I. Khanna, Jane.   II. Center for Strategic and International
   Studies (Washington, D.C.)   III. Series.
HC427.92.S634   1995
330.951'2—dc20   95-2896
                                                                  CIP

Contents

5

Ask a Tiger for Its Hide? Taiwan's Approaches to Economic Transactions across the Strait 61

Milton D. Yeh

6

Effect of the Natural Economic Territory on China's Economic and Political Strategies 71

Chen Dezhao

7

The Politics of Economic Integration among Taiwan, Hong Kong, and Southern China 82

Robert S. Ross

Tables and Figures

Foreword

East Asia today represents a fascinating combination of economic dynamism and political fragility. To be sure, exceptions exist. North Korea and Myanmar have persisted in pursuing ill-advised economic policies, resulting in a widening gap between them and others, but even they have recently signaled a desire for new economic policies.

On the political front also, differences can be discerned. Most of the members of the Association of Southeast Asian Nations (ASEAN) enjoy greater political stability than ever before. Nonetheless, throughout the region, with rare exceptions, political institutions are weak; hence, dependence on personalities is extensive. At this point, however, a generational change is under way throughout Asia, with new leaders about to be tested. Moreover, these new leaders will have to rely on performance, not charisma.

In this context, various trends toward greater economic interaction assume a special significance. To an unprecedented extent, economics dominates international relations today. Other issues, to be sure, exist. In some instances, territorial disputes cause tension; divided states constitute a special problem in East Asia; and ethnic and religious divisions also create crises. Yet in the day-to-day relations between and among nations, economic matters are in the forefront, profoundly influencing both domestic and foreign policies.

Much attention has been focused in the recent past on efforts to construct formal mechanisms and institutions so as to advance a more open and equitable marketplace and trading system. At the regional level, hopes in East Asia currently ride on the Asia-Pacific Economic Cooperation forum (APEC), an organization still in its formative period. ASEAN, a subregional body, has had a longer history than APEC, but its primary accomplishments thus far have been in the political rather than the economic realm. ASEAN has, however, established a timetable for a more open economic system among members, and APEC is also considering such a step. Meanwhile, at the global level, the World Trade Organization (WTO), successor to the General Agreement on Tariffs and Trade (GATT), faces a series of formidable tests in the period immediately ahead.

These organizations illustrate both the promise and the problem of institutions composed of sovereign states that seek to create commonly accepted rules for economic intercourse, rules often significantly affecting domestic policies. Although market-oriented economic systems have triumphed virtually everywhere over socialism, variations in cultural background, stage of development, and basic policies among such economies make the goal of harmonious coexistence a formidable challenge.

The essays in this volume deal with a different but at least equally important development in the international economic arena, namely, the emergence of natural economic territories (NETs). One important example is that of southern China—notably Guangdong and Fujian Provinces—Hong Kong, and Taiwan. NETs may be defined as economic entities that cut across political boundaries: pooling their resources, manpower, technology, and capital, they draw on the varied strengths of those involved. They can encompass portions of a nation-state as well as its entirety, but geographic proximity as well as cultural similarity constitute major assets.

NETs often require initial state support or, at a minimum, an absence of active opposition. Ultimately, however, they can only prosper if they are attractive to the private sector. They must have the elements that in combination represent a promising source of investment and market, fully competitive with other possibilities. NETs are not necessarily permanently fixed with respect to territory and participants. Depending on circumstances, enlargements can take place, with the initial locus serving as the base from which expansion occurs.

In essence, then, NETS represent a form of soft regionalism, one that evolves from the natural economic advantages present in given settings and is relatively unhampered by the need for separate political entities to reach a formal consensus on policies. Thus, in comparison with the existing supranational institutions, NETs advance economic intercourse more rapidly. And they have proliferated throughout East Asia as well as elsewhere. Many involve portions of the People's Republic of China: Fujian-Taiwan; Shandong-South Korea; the Tumen River delta, which involves Jilin, the northern extremity of North Korea, and the southern portion of the Siberian coast; and southwest China-Myanmar-Thailand-Vietnam. Yet NETs are in the process of being formed that relate to both Northeast and Southeast Asia apart from China: the Sea of Japan rim (referred to as the Eastern Sea by Korea) and South Thailand-Western Malaysia-Sumatra are examples.

As the essays here indicate, the political consequences of NETs are both important and complex. On the one hand, they raise difficult questions of control for the states involved. On this front as on many others, absolute state sovereignty is challenged. Moreover, they lead to a porousness, the consequences of which go far beyond the economic sphere to induce change in its broadest dimensions, even in states seeking to maintain authoritarian control over culture and politics.

NETs can also lead to tension in terms of intrastate relations or to a clash of perceived national interests. When a part of a state is drawn into a different and more dynamic external economic relationship, its relations with other parts of that state are affected, both positively and negatively. And when that relationship reaches a critical level, it may constitute leverage upon others, a worry that Taiwan authorities have expressed in terms of their involvement with southern China.

At the same time, intensive economic interaction raises the costs and risks of military conflict perceptibly. To take a notable example, China must give the most serious consideration to the consequences before it uses force either in the case of its differences with Taiwan or with the Southeast Asian states over the South China Sea atolls. A resort to force would have a devastating effect on its economy as well as on its general relations with all of the major nations. On balance, greater external economic involvement complicates the decision-making processes of all states, including authoritarian ones. And at the same time, it is a far swifter route to domestic change than an autarkic course.

The authors of the essays in this volume are to be commended for exploring the ramifications of NETs—economic, political, and strategic. They have provided us with new perspectives and raised issues that will require further research in the course of examining one of the intriguing new phenomena that mark this most revolutionary of times.

ROBERT A. SCALAPINO
Robson Research Professor of Government Emeritus
University of California, Berkeley

Preface

The emergence of subregional economies in the Asia-Pacific region and their impact on nation-state sovereignty was the focus of a two-year project that the Pacific Forum CSIS initiated in the fall of 1993. The project's concept posited that intense cross-border economic flows that link subregions of nation-states—or "natural economic territories" (NETs) as they have been termed by Robert Scalapino—have an important effect on the ability of central governments to manage their respective economic, political, and security interests in the post–cold war era when cooperation and competition are constantly vying to reshape Asia-Pacific relations.

We selected as the first case study in a series the southern China subregional economy, which links Hong Kong and Taiwan (formally, the Republic of China) with the People's Republic of China's southern coastal provinces of Guangdong and Fujian. Drawing a multidisciplinary group of experts together in the spring of 1993 in Hong Kong, we sought to examine relations among the three entities through the prism of the subregional economy, or NET. By adopting this narrow view of the interrelationships among the three, we hoped to capture points of rift and accord at the governmental and provincial levels when economic flows seem to outpace the central governments' ability to manage them.

The chapters in this volume serve as a reminder of the evolution of relations among the three governments since Special Economic Zones were introduced in Guangdong Province by Deng Xiaoping in 1979. The interrelationships among the three entities were relatively simple then in contrast to the present time: the "Basic Law" of Hong Kong was only in the conceptual stage, Taiwan had barely embarked on democratization and export-led policies, and mainland China had yet to fully adopt its "socialist market economy" dictum. The political and economic systems of each entity were anathema to each other, and economic flows across the Taiwan Strait and along the Hong Kong-mainland border were limited to small-time smugglers, largely ignored by the central governments.

By the start of 1995, relations among mainland China, Taiwan, and Hong Kong had become a great deal more complicated and rife with complexity—leadership transition was occurring in different forms in all three entities, economic development strategies vied increasingly with security and political goals, and Prime Minister Jiang Zemin's Lunar New Year speech was busily being interpreted either as an offer of accommodation to Taiwan or an indication of the confusion of coalition power-brokering in the emerging post-Deng era.

This volume does not attempt to address broad issues of relations among China, Taiwan, and Hong Kong. Rather, the authors offer perspectives on how interrelations have been facilitated by the evolution of the southern China regional economy—an experiment that all three entities have had to manage and grapple with during its 15-year evolution. The NET has wedded their economic destinies and, in so doing, has created internal and external dynamics that were unforeseen at the outset. Among the questions we asked of the authors were: What are the significant internal tensions, such as strains between the NET province(s) and the central government as well as among provinces? What leverage do governments have to address these strains, as well as such social problems as unequal distribution of gains, the new mobility of labor, and imported versus traditional values? Do governments possess adequate tools to channel, speed, or slow the pace of subregional economic interaction if they so choose? Does growing economic interdependence foster or help contain political conflict?

Each of the authors in this volume addresses the impact of the southern China NET from a different vantage point, reflecting distinct disciplines and national perspectives. In chapter 1, I blend discussion from the Hong Kong conference with additional research to provide an overview of how the NET has helped to shape internal central policy decisions in each entity, highlighting the tensions between the center and both provinces and business sectors. I also address the NET's impact on relations among the three entities and conclude that because the centers have been able to test economic reforms at the subregional level, they are able to test the political waters of easing tensions as well.

Sung Yun-wing in chapter 2 addresses the scope and pace of integration in the capital, commodity, services, and labor markets among the three entities, pointing out the competitive advantages and disadvantages of each vis-à-vis the specialization of each market. He includes a section on economic flows between Taiwan and Hong Kong, which have not received as much attention as cross-strait flows, and offers a new formula for estimating commodity trade between Taiwan and the mainland, an elusive task given that it is masked by Taipei's requirement that all shipping transit "third parties," notably Hong Kong. He concludes that integration will proceed unevenly, with the commodity markets progressing more quickly than the other sectors, which encounter stricter controls.

The role of overseas Chinese investment in the mainland China-Hong Kong-Taiwan NET is addressed in chapter 3, and Sally Stewart offers ample evidence that Chinese "compatriots"—not only in Hong Kong and Taiwan but in Southeast Asia as well—utilize their extensive family and ancestral networks in southern China as conduits for investment and trade. In this analysis, the entrepreneurial drive in this NET is a primary factor in its success, and the reader is led through a number of successful business partnerships that illustrate the importance of cultural affinity in producing efficient economic linkages.

Hong Kong officials are notable for their disdain for government interference in the marketplace, and J. A. Miller in chapter 4 offers a sobering reminder that governments should be in the business of opening their economies to the global economy and not bend to business sectors that are threatened by new sources of competition. In the Hong Kong case, he celebrates Deng Xiaoping's removal of unnatural barriers to trade in 1979 and argues that the sometimes-painful economic restructuring that has occurred in the intervening years has allowed Hong Kong to regain financial strength in its role as entrepôt for mainland China.

The perspective and analysis in chapter 5 differs distinctly from those of the previous chapters. Milton Yeh contends that the initiative from mainland China to increase cross-Taiwan Strait economic flows is a "risky business" for Taipei because it must deal with an "awakening lion" whose actions are unpredictable. The political aspects of this NET are clear in this analysis, as are the internal debates surrounding "acquiescing" to mainland China's advances. Yeh makes clear that there has been considerable political debate on the pace and scope of increased economic ties across the strait and on whether the economic benefits outweigh the political vulnerabilities for Taipei.

In chapter 6, Chen Dezhao addresses the challenges to Beijing in managing this NET, analyzing in particular how Beijing has attempted to redress the regional imbalances and "clashes" between coast and hinterland provinces that developed from the success of NET policies. He outlines the role of the NET in shaping Beijing's expansion of the southern China experiment and how Beijing has responded, particularly with a new set of economic policy adjustments announced in January 1994. This chapter highlights both Beijing's commitment to an open policy and its efforts to design an effective macroeconomic policy to govern the country while implementing economic decentralization. Moreso than the other papers—which examine relationships among the three NET entities—this chapter focuses on the ramifications of economic convergence within mainland China, in particular the internal subregional pressures and problems that Beijing has to face in managing its broader NET relationships.

The final chapter, by Robert Ross, addresses the question of whether intensified economic interdependence among the three entities of the NET reduces or creates new sources of political conflict. Ross portrays economic development strategies in the three entities within a broader context of national security policies. He argues that the political requirements of economic policy will govern future strategy and cautions Taiwan that its political advantage in engaging in the NET is on the wane.

I am deeply grateful to all of the authors for their time and commitment to this volume and to Amos Jordan and Robert Scalapino for their outstanding intellectual contributions to the series of NET case studies that the Pacific Forum is undertaking.

The Pacific Forum is also grateful to The Pew Charitable Trusts for its invaluable support of this two-year project and to the Institute of International Relations at National Chengchi University for its support of the case study in this volume.

JANE KHANNA
Honolulu, Hawaii

About the Contributors

Chen Dezhao is deputy chief and member of the executive board of the Division of International Economic Studies at the China Center for International Studies in Beijing.

Jane Khanna is assistant director for programs and development at the Pacific Forum CSIS in Honolulu. A graduate of The Johns Hopkins University Paul H. Nitze School of Advanced International Studies, she worked for the United Nations Development Program and the Social Science Research Council prior to joining the Forum in 1989.

J. A. Miller is director general of Hong Kong's Trade Department and is responsible for multilateral policy and North American bilateral relations. He is a graduate of the School of Oriental and African Studies in London and of the John F. Kennedy School of Government at Harvard University.

Robert S. Ross is a research associate at the John King Fairbank Center for East Asian Research, Harvard University, and was a visiting professor at the College of Foreign Affairs in Beijing during 1994–1995.

Sally Stewart is head of the Department of Management Studies at the University of Hong Kong and specializes in international marketing. She recently founded the Center of Ethics and Values at the University of Hong Kong. Ms. Stewart holds several degrees from Oxford University.

Sung Yun-wing is a reader in economics and codirector of the Hong Kong and Asia-Pacific Economies Research Programme at the Chinese University of Hong Kong. A widely published author, he is also corresponding editor of *Asian Pacific Economic*

Literature. His research interests cover international trade and economic development in China, Hong Kong, and Taiwan.

Milton D. (Ming-deh) Yeh is a research fellow at the Institute of International Relations at National Chengchi University in Taipei. He was the recipient of a Fulbright grant in 1993. His research interests include politics in mainland China and Hong Kong. He earned a Ph.D. in political science from the University of Pittsburgh.

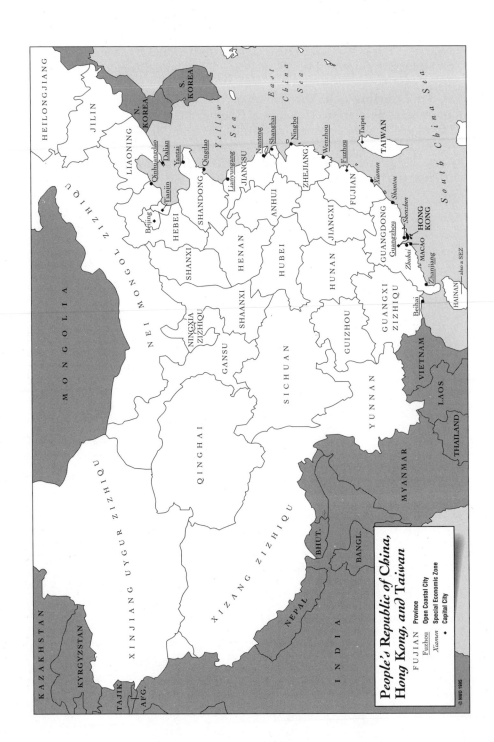

People's Republic of China, Hong Kong, and Taiwan

FUJIAN — Province
Fuzhou — Open Coastal City
Xiamen — Special Economic Zone
♦ — Capital City

© NWD 1995

KAZAKHSTAN

KYRGYZSTAN

TAJIK.

AFG.

MONGOLIA

NEI MONGOL ZIZHIQU

XINJIANG UYGUR ZIZHIQU

XIZANG ZIZHIQU

QINGHAI

GANSU

NINGXIA ZIZHIQU

SHAANXI

SICHUAN

YUNNAN

GUIZHOU

GUANGXI ZIZHIQU

HUNAN

HUBEI

HENAN

SHANXI

HEBEI

SHANDONG

Beijing

Tianjin

Qinhuangdao

Dalian

Yantai

Qingdao

Lianyungang

JIANGSU

Nantong

Shanghai

Ningbo

Wenzhou

ZHEJIANG

ANHUI

JIANGXI

FUJIAN

Fuzhou

Xiamen

Shantou

GUANGDONG

Guangzhou

Shenzhen

Zhuhai

MACAO

HONG KONG

Zhanjiang

Beihai

HAINAN — also a SEZ

HEILONGJIANG

JILIN

LIAONING

N. KOREA

S. KOREA

Yellow Sea

East China Sea

South China Sea

Taipei

TAIWAN

MONGOLIA

MYANMAR

VIETNAM

LAOS

THAILAND

INDIA

NEPAL

BHUT.

BANGL.

xvi

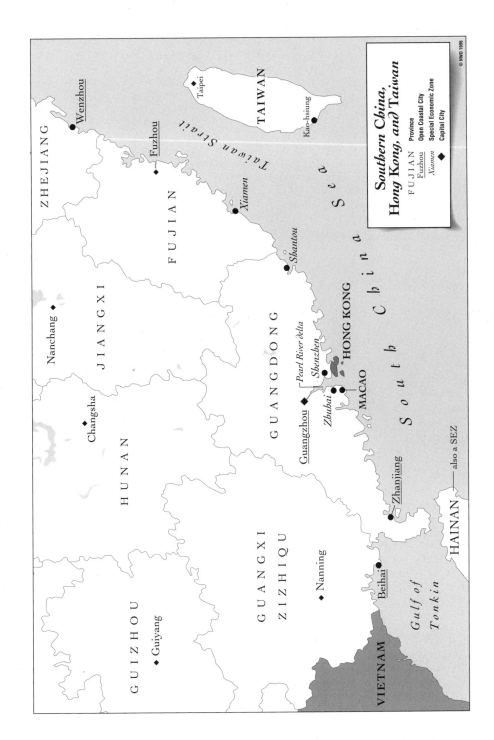

ZHEJIANG

Wenzhou

JIANGXI

Nanchang

FUJIAN

Fuzhou

Xiamen

Shantou

TAIWAN

Taipei

Kao-hsiung

Taiwan Strait

HUNAN

Changsha

GUANGDONG

Pearl River Delta

Shenzhen

Guangzhou

Zhuhai

MACAO

HONG KONG

South China Sea

GUIZHOU

Guiyang

GUANGXI
ZIZHIQU

Nanning

Zhanjiang

HAINAN — also a SEZ

Beihai

Gulf of
Tonkin

VIETNAM

© NWD 1995

*Southern China,
Hong Kong, and Taiwan*

FUJIAN   Province
Fuzhou   Open Coastal City
Xiamen   Special Economic Zone
◆   Capital City

xvii

1

The Calculus of Interests in the Subregional Economy of Southern China, Hong Kong, and Taiwan

Jane Khanna

The dynamic economic growth in the Asia-Pacific region is giving rise to a new type of economic development strategy in
which subregions of nation-states together harness their complementary endowments across political borders. Variously
called "natural economic territories" (NETs), "growth circles,"
or "growth triangles," the phenomenon is marked by an intensified movement of capital, labor, goods, and technology among
contiguous localities of three or more countries.[1] Although
trade among neighbors is certainly not new, the emerging
breadth and depth of economic interaction among various subregions has led some to argue that trade boundaries are blur-
ring political boundaries. Indeed, in some cases, subregions of
nation-states are developing economic links with neighbors that
may be becoming more vital than their links with the political
centers of power that govern them. This has raised the question
of whether there is an emerging disjuncture between economic
relations generated "from below" and political authority admin-
istered "from above."

Nowhere are these questions more relevant than in the subregional economy that has developed among Hong Kong, Taiwan, and the provinces of Guangdong and Fujian in the
southern region of the People's Republic of China. The impressive economic performance along China's southeastern coast has
received wide attention since its Special Economic Zones (SEZs)
started to fuel growth in the early 1980s. As the decade ended,
capital and other inputs from Taiwan and Hong Kong, as well as
from other overseas Chinese communities, had created an economic boom that had swept across political borders, thoroughly
transforming the respective economies in the process. As one
contributor in this volume observes, it is striking that a market of
such huge proportions has developed without a single meeting,
discussion, or negotiation about its growth among officials of
these areas.[2]

Yet the absence of a coordinated policy framework among the governments of this NET reflects the explicit, opposing political and security agendas of each entity in pursuing the NET: for China, reunification with Taiwan and the assertion of its interests in Hong Kong leading up to 1997; for Taiwan, de facto independence from China and a legitimate and autonomous international role; and for Hong Kong, maximization of its importance to the Chinese economy in order to deter political or economic retrenchment by Beijing, post-1997. This NET has thus progressed through a series of *unilateral* economic policies that seek to advance and protect the political and security agendas of the three entities in a dynamic process that no one of them fully controls.

Clearly, increased economic interdependence has helped to modernize each of the economies, thereby enhancing state power.[3] Yet ultimately this interdependence may well have exacerbated rather than lessened security concerns: the governments of China and Taiwan are each particularly wary that their economies should not become hostage to the other's political goals. In part, this is because economic ties have resulted in an unanticipated compromise of central policy control over increasing segments of their respective economies—less a concern in Hong Kong than in China and Taiwan.

The analysis below first offers an overview of the domestic tensions created in each of the entities over participation in the NET and then turns to the importance of the NET to each entity's ability to manage its interests.

Domestic Tensions in Mainland China

Internal tensions on the mainland over development of the southern China NET are illustrated by the ongoing struggle between Beijing and Guangdong Province over autonomy and control issues, by provincial demands for favorable economic privileges and benefits, and by Beijing's concern over growing linkages between Guangdong and Fujian and Hong Kong and Taiwan. This interplay of relations—center-province, intraprovince, and provincial—with external actors has become increasingly complex in the evolution of China's 15-year experiment with economic reforms.

The 1979 devolution of many economic powers from the central government to Guangdong saw a renewal of Guangdong's historical role as a gateway to the south, which had long inspired a local spirit and identity that Beijing had sought to subjugate. This marked a departure from decades of tight political control—wielded by trusted officials appointed from the center—and a central government policy that allocated little investment to the province after the shift of industrial production from the coastal areas to the interior for security reasons following the Korean War. It was thus Guangdong's minor importance to the national economy, in addition to its historical gateway role, that made it an attractive arena in which to experiment with risky economic reforms and a place where damage could be limited if reforms failed.[4]

Deng Xiaoping thus chose Guangdong as an initial focus of his 1979 economic reforms and his plans to develop economic ties with Hong Kong and Taiwan—with the tacit goal of preparing them for reunification with the mainland. Guangdong's three-decade-long subjugation to national priorities had generated a pent-up demand for economic betterment, reflected in the statement of one provincial party secretary that Guangdong would develop much faster if it were an independent nation.[5] Yet the province's quest for greater autonomy was only possible when its goals converged with those of the central government leadership, which itself was divided between pro-reformers and conservatives who "tried in turn to protect and oppose Guangdong's reforms."[6]

While provincial officials molded their strategies according to political currents in the central government, Beijing authorities widened economic reforms—to speed and broaden economic growth; to offset the growing dominance of the southern Chinese economy, with its concomitant push toward political autonomy; and to appease demands from other areas, such as Shanghai, that contended for preferential treatment as early as 1980. As one scholar observed,

> The central government would have growing difficulties in decentralizing more power to Guangdong over time because one province after another has been demanding similar treatment. Not only did this competition for more power cut into the central government's own position but it also allowed many other areas to share Guangdong's once monopolized privileges by the early 1990s and become its keen competitors.[7]

Over time, then, Beijing's economic reform policies resulted in a widespread decentralization of decision making, which was intended not only to spur economic development but also to disperse decision-making powers to a variety of regional authorities so as to preclude one region or province from growing too strong in relation to others. By devolving power not just to provincial authorities but to a diversity of actors—including village and township enterprises—Beijing generated economic and political competition at the regional level, avoiding any "simple struggle for control between center and province."[8] This regional competition serves Beijing's interests by giving more actors a stake in the success of economic reforms, but it is also witness to how difficult it is to contain the genie of reform once it is released.

Thus, as Beijing loosened economic controls, its ability to enforce economic policies when it needed to steadily eroded. There are few institutional mechanisms in Beijing's nascent economic infrastructure to manage such a devolution of power. In addition to lacking adequate monetary, fiscal, and administrative levers to implement its overall policy decrees, Beijing is proving to be weak in mediating interprovincial conflicts, which have dramatically increased, particularly between the richer coastal provinces and the hinterland. And the center's ability to rein in provincial autonomy has also weakened; Guangdong in recent years, for example, has been able to resist Beijing's efforts to appoint its local officials, and it has also been successful in negotiating a reduced payment to the center's coffers, both matters of historical contention between the provinces and the center.[9] The fact that Beijing-directed economic reforms have coincided with succession struggles in the central government has meant that provincial officials are reluctant to concede powers to or make sacrifices for a central government whose current political composition may not last very long.[10]

One Chinese scholar has observed that "the south China NET symbolizes a window for other parts of China to see the outside world and explore ways to converge with the world market and the global economy."[11] This dynamic has proliferated, of course, with the progressive regionalization of the mainland economy. China is involved, currently or prospectively, in a number of additional NETs: the Golden Quadrangle that encompasses parts of northern Thailand, Yunnan Province in China, northern Myanmar, and Laos; Hunchun in the northeast; and the Yellow Sea or Bohai, also in the northeast. Given the variety of regions and nations thus linked with China and the widely varying nature and intensity of the interdependencies involved,

China's neighbors will increasingly be called on to deal with its peripheries rather than the center in economic relations. This will require a more differentiated understanding of China and thus provides an area for further research.[12]

Domestic Tensions in Taiwan

Internal divisions in Taiwan over the pace and scope of economic opening to the mainland have developed with increasing intensity since China unilaterally ended its ban on Taiwanese investment and trade in 1979. It took Taipei six years to reciprocate and in 1985 lift its own ban on trade and investment with the mainland, and then only with strict regulations that it has very gradually eased in the years since.

The debates surrounding economic relations with the mainland are of both a political and an economic nature, and they exist inside Taiwan's government agencies and business sectors as well as between the two—in other words, the topic has become all-pervasive. The most divisive issues concern establishing direct transportation links with the mainland and further liberalization of trade, investment, and people flows, including an investment agreement that would provide legal protection to Taiwanese investors. Although the government is anxious not to create economic dependencies on the mainland that would compromise its pursuit of a legitimate and autonomous international role, business is eager to overcome the increased costs and inconvenience of operating its mainland trade and investment through third parties, notably Hong Kong. This is particularly true for the financial and transportation conglomerates, whose investments are large and long term, thus requiring the greater legal protection and transparency that can only be embodied in intergovernmental agreements with the mainland.

Yet the small and medium-sized businesses—which make up the overwhelming bulk of Taiwan's trade and investment in the southern China coastal provinces—seek short-term profits offered by the mainland's low production costs and large market, and they seem to trade and invest almost regardless of their own government's policies.[13] This mobility of people, capital, and goods despite government restrictions in part capitalizes on Taiwan's historical, cultural, and linguistic linkages with Fujian Province. Government restrictions have in part been designed to prevent a "hollowing out" of Taiwan's industrial structure, but they have also been motivated by a fear that the mainland authorities might at some point squeeze Taiwanese businesses heavily invested in China to extract political benefits.

The political debates surrounding economic relations with the mainland are informed by Taiwan's growing economic wealth and a demographic shift toward Taiwanese-born citizens, which has created a large middle class that favors increased independence from the mainland. The majority of Taiwanese favor de facto rather than formal independence, but the rising Democratic People's Party (DPP), with its platform of formal independence, effectively competes with the ruling Kuomintang (KMT) on this issue. Partly as a result, the government has sought a higher international profile to satisfy proponents of de facto independence and to weaken the appeal of elements seeking formal independence. To enhance its profile and to develop an alternative to increasing interdependence with the mainland, in early 1994 Taipei launched a "southern strategy" to develop political and economic relations with Southeast Asia.[14]

Contrary to observations that the southern strategy is an attempt to offset growing dependence on the mainland, Taipei officials maintain that it is part of a long-term goal of developing Taiwan as a regional transport and service center, which in its most ambitious form envisions Taiwan as a hub linking Singapore and Shanghai and which would attract multinational firms to locate their headquarters in Taiwan. In addition, by encouraging Taiwan firms to relocate to places like Singapore rather than Hong Kong or mainland China, Taipei hopes to further internationalize its key industries and create linkages with the growth industries in Southeast Asia.[15] Taipei views this plan as an effort to internationalize its economic relations without detracting from the advantages that accrue from its proximity to the mainland; an increased economic presence in Southeast Asia may also provide a way for Taipei to check the mainland's influence in the countries of the Association of Southeast Asian Nations (ASEAN). This plan also provides a vehicle by which to expand and strengthen the financial and service sectors—particularly telecommunications and transportation—which need to take center stage in further modernizing the Taiwan economy and maintaining the global competitiveness of its manufacturing industries.

After two years of study and debate, the Taiwan government announced in January 1995 the approval of a blueprint to move forward with the "hub plan," which includes the establishment of an offshore transportation center in southwest Kao-hsiung

Harbor that would be allowed to ship to the mainland. The hub plan, arguably the most ambitious in four decades, would create six specialized centers to attract multinational operations in key industrial sectors. It would also require a major overhaul of the country's legal and regulatory systems, as well as liberalization of its financial, communications, and immigration policies. Given the conflicting views about closer ties with the mainland—within business, government, and the DPP—the "Singapore-Taipei-Shanghai hub" plan remains controversial.[16] The Legislative Yuan must approve many of the rule changes and was on a timeline to do so by mid-1995 for the plan to proceed on schedule. The legislative debate will not be made easier by at least one indication of approval from a mainland official for the hub plan,[17] which makes it easier for the DPP to argue that the plan plays into the mainland's opportunistic policy of reunification through economic integration rather than military force. The KMT's proponents of the plan will need to argue that the plan keeps Taiwan on the offensive economically, thus increasing its political leverage vis-à-vis the mainland.

Yet the internal contradictions in each of these stances will become increasingly difficult to defend. The DPP, which altogether avoided mentioning the independence issue in the December 1993 elections in order to appeal to mainstream voters, will risk popular support should it try to thwart the hub plan by arguing for an independent political path. The ruling KMT will need to keep the economic gains of its hub plan at the forefront, yet in doing so it risks compromising its stated political position of "no contact, no trade, no direct transportation," which has been steadily chipped away, only most recently by the hub plan itself. The hub plan thus requires each party to mask its official stance and thus has great implications for their political legitimacy among a diversified and newly empowered electorate.

Hong Kong

Hong Kong's involvement in the NET has created internal divisions different from those in Taiwan and China. There is little disagreement among government and business sectors that economic expansion into Guangdong Province—which has extended broadly into the Pearl River delta area—has benefited the economy and will continue to do so after 1997. As one Hong Kong official has observed, "Trade is like water; when barriers are lifted it finds its own natural course."[18]

Yet concerns have been expressed recently that the absence of any rule of law in southern China's frenetic business world could infect Hong Kong as well.[19] Rather than Guangdong being an extension of Hong Kong, as now appears the case, the reverse may also occur, and Beijing's weak enforcement of laws and rules in the south may spill into Hong Kong. Moreover, should there be a shift of emphasis away from Guangdong to Shanghai in the post-Deng period, as some reports indicate, Hong Kong could be adversely affected by lack of clout at the political center.

Beijing's stated commitment of "one country, two systems" in the post-1997 period is at the heart of the pro-democracy and pro-Beijing factions that have been gnawing at the political and social fabric of the city-state for several years. The issue of Hong Kong's democratization is not, of course, driven by participation in the NET but rather by the pace and scope of Governor Christopher Patten's speeded-up attempt to broaden political representation before July 1, 1997.

Yet interactions between China and Hong Kong over democratization in the latter end up being conditioned by economic interdependence in the NET. Despite its threats, Beijing has been unable to halt the democratization process in Hong Kong. Hong Kong's power derives from its central role in the growth of southern China, whose development in turn is key for the entire Chinese economy. By promoting its entrepôt role and restructuring as a service hub for southern China, Hong Kong hopes that— in combination with its allies and partners in Guangdong—it will be able to resist Beijing's pressures. Beijing, in turn, is constrained from acting too vigorously by its need to demonstrate that it can manage "diversity" in the post-1997 period. Should it react too harshly against a Hong Kong trying to preserve its democratic reforms, it would risk disturbing the political stability and economic dynamism that are key to Hong Kong's prosperity. If China fails this test, it could jeopardize Taiwan's return as well. Again, the outcome of Beijing's leadership succession struggle will influence how these matters are resolved.

Impact of the NET on Relations among the Entities

Has the southern China subregional economy compromised management by the central governments of their respective economic, political, and security interests? Some scholars argue that the southern China NET is being driven by uncontrollable entrepreneurial linkages while the central governments are

passive if unhappy onlookers. Although it was clearly the
Beijing government's policy of Special Economic Zones that
first unleashed cross-border flows, Deng did not envision the
extent of economic opening that these zones would create, this
argument goes, and would not have gone down this path if he
had. Other scholars argue that security concerns are paramount
in this NET and that the extensive cross-border flows are politically motivated by Beijing's reunification aspirations, with
Hong Kong and Taipei on the disadvantageous receiving end.
In other words, this NET exists only at the pleasure of the governments' security interests, which are primarily in Beijing's
favor.

In many ways, the first argument is a convincing one. This
NET is a clear example of economic relations generated from
"below," creating a momentum increasingly independent of the
political authority of the respective central governments. The
SEZs in the southern China coastal area helped to give the Taiwan and Hong Kong economies a new lease on life and allowed
them to restructure and gain competitiveness as well as international stature in ways unforeseen by Beijing. The vitality of the
southern China subregional economy is thus not principally due
to government policies or to political goals but to the existence of
locally driven economic complementarities that have a life of
their own. The three governments realize that should they
attempt to again constrict the vast movements of people, goods,
and capital out of security concerns, there would emerge a
smuggling enterprise impossible to control, both across the strait
and across the Hong Kong-mainland border. These extralegal,
chaotic economic transactions would be equally intolerable for
their respective security interests, not to mention the economic
welfare costs that would jeopardize economic modernization
and even political stability.

Yet the governments have proved that they are not passive
spectators either. The development of the subregional economy
has thrust the central governments into the role of balancing the
conflicting domestic forces of economic liberalization and political "protectionism," in many ways enhancing rather than diminishing their economic and political functions. In this facilitator
role, the governments have demonstrated their ability to rechan-
nel economic flows among their subregions when their interests
are threatened, reflected by the increasing regionalization of the
mainland economy, the southern strategy that Taipei has
embarked upon, and Hong Kong's redoubled efforts to serve as

the most efficient gateway to China, thus empowering its political role.

These efforts to offset the possible deleterious effects of over-reliance on one province and its ties to external actors have had their own consequences and have presented new challenges of economic decentralization to central government leadership. And these challenges come at a sensitive time for leadership transition in all three entities: a democratizing Taiwan in which native Taiwanese are grasping the reins of power for the first time; the emergence of coalitions rather than individual charismatic leaders in the post-Deng era; and an economically vibrant if politically confused Hong Kong with no guarantees for a voice in its own destiny after July 1997.

What, then, is the importance of the southern China NET to relations among the central governments? In significant ways, this NET no longer serves as a barometer of these relations, as it did even five years ago; each government's interaction in this subregional economy has been diffused by the economy's very success, because each government now seeks to replicate or off-set its economic importance in other subregions.

There are, however, two important lessons. First, for Taipei and Beijing, the NET has allowed governments that are actively hostile toward each other to interact and test the political waters of easing tensions. In this 15-year experiment, there have been no breakthroughs; China has not renounced its "right of force" should Taiwan claim independence, and the Taipei government has been emboldened to seek an independent international profile, such as by joining the General Agreement on Tariffs and Trade and the United Nations—policies that still put the two governments on a collision course. Yet the NET probably did lead to the first direct interactions between the two governments in four decades of hostilities, and despite lack of any agreements in three meetings, there is commitment on both sides to continue to try.[20] As argued elsewhere in this volume, economic interdependence between the two has possibly delayed extreme conflict and "motivated a search for negotiated solutions" on lesser sources of conflict.[21]

The second lesson, perhaps more applicable to other nation-states, is the lesson that the Beijing and Taipei governments have been forced to learn: how to devise an economic development strategy that involves a growing private sector and provincial leadership in a context of tremendous political sensitivity. Arguably, the mainland has been floundering at this task compared with Taipei—perhaps understandably given the enormity of Beijing's task. Yet the economic success of the southern China NET has had an important demonstration effect that continues to inform both governments of the pitfalls and benefits of economic decentralization, whether it be in a "social market system" or an avowedly capitalist one.

The political evolution in each of these entities is at a watershed and will dramatically affect relations among them. Yet the mainland China-Hong Kong-Taiwan NET shows that hostile political entities can learn to interact on an economic plane without changing their own political ground rules—when it is in their interest to do so. Although it could be that in some circumstances the governments might want to limit or slow the NET flows, current policy in all three governments is to expand and strengthen, not dismantle, the NET, demonstrating its overall utility to them.

Conclusions

Perhaps nowhere in Asia are economic and security strategies more intertwined than among Beijing, Taipei, and Hong Kong. Although their economic liberalization policies are never far removed from their political goals, the vitality of cross-border linkages in the southern China NET has compelled revision upon revision of central government strategies. The development of the southern China NET should thus be viewed as a historic and crucial development for these governments' internal and external affairs, because it has provided a testing ground for both internal economic and external political strategies.

All three entities are diversifying their economic activities away from this NET—Hong Kong into the Pearl River delta, Taiwan into Southeast Asia and Shanghai, and mainland China into all of its vast borderlands. The southern China subregional economy will therefore be less of a focal point for interrelations than in the past. Yet it will proceed to develop, with continual jostling between the provinces and the center, with continued economic and political strains among the provinces, and with further economic integration of Guangdong and Fujian within the NET and with regional and international markets.

In interstate relations, the significance of this NET lies not in the prospect that it has or can resolve these entities' most entrenched security conflict—namely, sovereignty—but in its capacity as a confidence-building measure that has provided limited ways for these governments to cooperate at the margins of this conflict. The southern China-Taiwan-Hong Kong NET is unlikely to resolve age-old animosities among the respective parties; in fact, it might even help to revive them. Still, to the degree that it offers economic incentives to abandon old psychological patterns of distrust for new patterns of cooperation, it should be constructive rather than divisive. Although the intimacy of NETs could create new forms of conflict, the interdependencies this phenomenon has produced increase the cost of political conflict and create greater stakes in political cooperation than competition.

Notes

1. This chapter draws extensively on an article by the author and Amos A. Jordan entitled "Economic Interdependence and the Nation-State: The Emergence of Natural Economic Territories in the Asia Pacific," *Journal of International Affairs* 48, no.2 (Winter 1995): 433–462.

The term "natural economic territory" was coined by Robert A. Scalapino in "The United States and Asia: Future Prospects," *Foreign Affairs* 70, no. 5 (Winter 1991–92): 19–40.

2. See chapter 3.

3. For further arguments, see chapter 6.

4. Peter Tsan-yin Cheung, "The Case of Guangdong in Central-Provincial Relations," in Jia Hao and Lin Zhimin, eds., *Changing Central-Local Relations in China: Reform and State Capacity* (Boulder, Colo.: Westview Press, 1994), 207–237; and Peter T. Y. Cheung, "Relations between the Central Government and Guangdong," in Y. M. Yeung and David K. Y. Chu, eds., *Guangdong: Survey of a Province Undergoing Rapid Change* (Hong Kong: The Chinese University Press, 1994), 20–51.

5. Cheung, "Relations between the Central Government and Guangdong," 8.

6. Ibid., 30.

7. Ibid., 25. This policy of further opening was most recently expanded in Deng Xiaoping's famous "southern tour" in the spring of 1992 that resulted in 14 "open" (liberalized trade) zones along the coastal belt and extended economic reform privileges to more than 330 localities in nearly every corner of the country.

8. Gerald Segal, "China Changes Shape: Regionalism and Foreign Policy," *Adelphi Paper 287* (London: International Institute for Strategic Studies, March 1994), 55.

9. Cheung, "Relations between the Central Government and Guangdong," 41.

10. Segal, "China Changes Shape," 55.

11. See chapter 4.

12. Segal, "China Changes Shape."

13. Osman Tseng, "Risky Business," *Free China Review* 44, no. 1 (January 1994): 34–35.

14. Pursuing this strategy was the primary purpose for President Lee Teng-hui's highly publicized Southeast Asia "vacation tour" in early 1994.

15. See Deborah Shen, "Singapore key in ROC Trade Plan," *Free China Journal*, January 13, 1995, p. 7.

16. The intergovernmental controversies, for example, are often between the Ministry of Economic Affairs, which takes a more liberal view toward increased linkages with the mainland, and the Ministry of Foreign Affairs and the Mainland Affairs Council, which are more conservative. See Eugenia Yun, "The Billion NT Dollar Question," *Free China Review* 44, no. 1 (January 1994): 16–23, especially 23.

17. Frank Ching, "Taiwan Looks for Loopholes," *Far Eastern Economic Review*, February 2, 1995, p. 29.

18. See chapter 4.

19. Louise do Rosario, "Risky Business," *Far Eastern Economic Review*, January 26, 1995, p. 20.

20. These were the Koo-Wang talks between Taiwan's Koo Chen-fu, chairman of the Straits Exchange Foundation (SEF), and China's Wang Dao-han, chairman of the Association for Relations Across the Taiwan Straits (ARATS). The SEF was established in February 1991 and ARATS in December 1991 to serve as intermediary bodies for inter-strait talks. The first talks were held in Singapore in April 1993 and subsequently in November 1993 and March 1994. The two sides could not even agree, however, on the limited agenda items of repatriation of illegal immigrants and hijackers and cross-strait fishing disputes.

Plans for a second round of Koo-Wang talks were suspended in July 1995 by Beijing in protest against the United States' granting of a visa to Taiwan's president, Lee Teng-hui.

21. See chapter 6.

2

Patterns of Economic Interdependence in the Natural Economic Territory

Sung Yun-wing

The inauguration of the People's Republic of China's open door policy and economic reforms in 1979 has created a dynamic natural economic territory (NET) among Taiwan, Hong Kong, and the provinces of Fujian and Guangdong that has substantially affected world trade and investment.[1] The special policy packages that Beijing granted to Guangdong and Fujian vastly increased their autonomy in managing foreign trade and investment and gave them the authority to operate Special Economic Zones (SEZs). These policies coincided with severe labor shortages in Hong Kong and Taiwan and the need for these economies to restructure, and thus facilitated the large-scale movement of export and labor- intensive industries from Hong Kong and Taiwan to the two Chinese provinces.

This chapter addresses the factors influencing integration among the NET entities as well as obstacles to and prospects for further integration. I first outline some fundamentals of economic interdependence among the NET entities, turning then to some of the obstacles to economic interaction among them. I analyze investment among the trio, reflecting integration of the financial and capital markets; trade among the trio, reflecting integration in the commodity markets; and flows of labor among the trio, crucial to integration of the labor markets. Finally, I discuss the prospects for their economic integration with one another.

Patterns of Interdependence

The mainland and Hong Kong economies are highly integrated, reflected by the fact that they are each other's foremost partners in both trade and investment. Despite the absence of official ties, economic integration has proceeded extremely rapidly between the mainland and Taiwan, largely utilizing the efficient intermediary services of Hong Kong.

Table 2.1
Southern China, Hong Kong, and Taiwan: Basic Indicators, 1992

Indicators	Hong Kong	Taiwan	Macao	Guang-dong	Fujian	Total
Area (sq. kilometers)	1,068	35,961	17	177,901	12,000	226,947
Population (millions)	5.8	20.8	0.37	64.6	31.2	122.8
Total GDP (U.S.$ billions)	95.6	206.6	4.6	41.6	12.5	–
Per capita GDP (U.S.$)	16,444	10,003	12,500	644	402	–
GDP growth rate (percentage)	5.3	6.5	3.1	19.5	21.7	–
Exports (U.S.$ billions)	118.6[a] 30.0[b]	81.4	1.8	33.4[c] 18.4[d]	– 4.1[d]	–

[a] Total exports (including reexports).
[b] Domestic exports.
[c] China customs statistics.
[d] MOFERT (Ministry of Foreign Economic Relations and Trade, Beijing) statistics. (Exports from processing operations are valued according to processing fees rather than value of output.)

Table 2.1 shows the basic economic indicators of this NET. The gross domestic product (GDP) of Taiwan is more than twice that of Hong Kong. Guangdong's 1992 exports of $33.4 billion surpassed the domestic exports of Hong Kong of $30 billion and, for comparison, Thailand's exports of $32 billion. Fujian was a distant second to Guangdong in terms of economic strength. Fujian's 1992 population of 31 million was nearly half of Guangdong's and its GDP was nearly a third smaller. The gap between them in trade and foreign investment is even greater. Fujian's 1992 exports and utilized foreign direct investment (FDI) were only 22 and 24 percent of Guangdong's respectively.

In 1991, Taiwan surpassed Hong Kong and the United States to become the second-largest supplier of goods to the mainland after Japan, and it also surpassed the United States and Japan to become the second-largest investor on the mainland after Hong Kong. In 1992, the mainland surpassed Japan to become the second-largest market for Taiwan's exports after the United States.

Although economic relations between Hong Kong and Guangdong, Taiwan and Fujian, and Hong Kong and Taiwan are quite close, relations between Guangdong and Fujian are not particularly strong. The provinces lack economic complementarity; neither is endowed with natural resources, and both are at similar stages of economic development. Further, each has a link to a different community of overseas Chinese, and these communities have different dialects and distinct origins in the two provinces. The two provinces compete for overseas markets and also for Taiwanese investment. Guangdong operates three SEZs: the Shenzhen and Zhuhai SEZs, which are adjacent to Hong Kong and Macao respectively, and the Shantou SEZ, which has close links to overseas Chinese populations, including a community in Hong Kong that originated in Shantou. Fujian operates the Xiamen SEZ opposite Taiwan. A majority of Taiwanese originated from Fujian, and Taiwan has accounted for the bulk of the FDI in Fujian. Yet, the prime destination of Taiwanese investment in China is Guangdong because its economic strength, investment environment, and infrastructure are far superior to those of Fujian.

Overcoming the Barriers to Economic Integration

Despite the intensive trade and investment flows, there are important obstacles to a deepening of economic integration. The foremost barrier is the mainland's command economy, which by its nature is designed to be insulated from the global economy and therefore finds it difficult to benefit from international trade and investment. A command economy tends to have an overvalued and inconvertible currency, which is a significant obstacle to international economic integration. Moreover, it is extremely difficult for the planners of a command economy to know what goods should be exported or imported because the economy tends to have a highly distorted and arbitrary price system. East-West trade is thus typically characterized as "asymmetric integration" because it involves the interaction of two economic systems that are functionally very different.

Institutional Barriers

Given the lack of diplomatic and formal commercial ties between the mainland and Taiwan, there is an obvious lack of institutional integration between them. Due to Taiwan's ban on direct business deals with the mainland, China and Taiwan are institutionally more closely integrated with most other economies than with each other.

Apart from the lack of diplomatic and commercial ties, the three important institutional barriers to economic integration often listed in textbooks are tariffs, controls on factor movements, and exchange risks. On these three counts, the barriers to economic integration among the mainland, Taiwan, and Hong Kong are very high. For instance, it is specified in the Sino-British Agreement on Hong Kong that it will remain a separate customs territory and will continue to have its own currency in the post-1997 period, and migration from China to Hong Kong will still be strictly controlled. It can be argued therefore that, even after 1997, Hong Kong and the mainland will be less institutionally integrated than Greece and Ireland, which as members of the European Union enjoy complete freedom of movement of goods and factors. Members of the European Monetary System within the Union are even more closely integrated because of their pegged exchange rates. Because China is not a member of the World Trade Organization (WTO) and the Chinese currency is not convertible, Hong Kong is institutionally more closely integrated with most of the economies of the free world than with China.

Integration via Cultural Affinity

Although economic theory concentrates on tariffs, controls on migration, and exchange integration, the effect of geographical proximity and cultural affinity may be even more important. Geographic and cultural proximity can enable businessmen to evade formal barriers to trade and investment. Tariffs can be evaded through smuggling, and smuggling from Hong Kong and Taiwan to China is rampant. The movement of people from Hong Kong and Taiwan to China is relatively free, although movement in the other direction is highly controlled. Illegal immigrants from the mainland are quite common in Hong Kong and Taiwan, however, because the labor markets in the two economies are extremely tight.

Unilateral Policy Changes

Unilateral policy changes are also important in the integration of the trio and, in China's case, are motivated by the desire to build closer links with both Hong Kong and Taiwan. Taiwanese businesses enjoy more special concessions in China than any other overseas businesses. Taiwanese goods face lower taxes in China, and import controls on Taiwanese goods are less stringent. A 1988 State Council decree gave Taiwanese investors favorable treatment over other foreign investors.[2] Local authorities also tend to give Taiwanese investors more favorable treatment in terms of faster approvals and better supporting services.

Although the mainland is more open to Taiwan than to any other economy, Taiwan is less open to the mainland than to other economies. Taiwan's import controls on mainland products have been gradually liberalized since 1987, and indirect imports of 92 items were allowed by the end of 1990. In July 1987, Taiwan eased its foreign exchange controls, and Taiwanese businesses began to invest indirectly on the mainland via subsidiaries established in Hong Kong or elsewhere. In November of that year, Taiwan allowed its citizens to visit their mainland relatives, and the number of Taiwanese visitors to the mainland soared. In October 1989, Taiwan promulgated regulations sanctioning indirect trade, investment, and technical cooperation with China. Taiwan's policy still requires that all trade, investment, and visits must be conducted indirectly—that is, via Hong Kong or elsewhere. Taiwan still prohibits investment from the mainland, although it is reported that the mainland has invested in Taiwan through its overseas subsidiaries.

On paper, Hong Kong businesses receive no more favorable concessions in China than other overseas businesses, yet in reality, Hong Kong businesses have a significant advantage because of geographical proximity and kinship links. Like Taiwan businesses, Hong Kong investors enjoy favorable concessions from Guangdong local authorities as a result of the kinship network. It is also easier for Hong Kong Chinese to visit the mainland than foreigners because they do not need visas. China is thus more open to Hong Kong than to other economies. Although Hong Kong, as a free economy, is open to the whole world including China, its controls on visitors from the mainland are stricter than its controls on visitors from other places due to a fear of illegal immigrants from China. In cooperation with Hong Kong, Beijing also imposes strict controls on its citizens' visits to Hong Kong.

Table 2.2
Contracted Foreign Investment in China by Source, 1979–1992
(in millions of U.S. dollars)

	1979–1990	1991	1992	1979–1992
National total	45,244 (100)	12,422 (100)	58,736 (100)	116,402 (100)
Hong Kong	26,480 (58.0)	7,531 (60.6)	40,502 (69.0)	74,513 (64.0)
Taiwan	2,000 (4.4)	1,392 (11.2)	5,548 (9.4)	8,968 (7.7)
United States	4,476 (9.9)	555 (4.5)	3,142 (5.3)	8,163 (7.0)
Japan	3,662 (8.1)	886 (7.1)	2,200 (3.7)	6,748 (5.8)

Source: Almanac of China's Foreign Economic Relations and Trade (Beijing), various issues.

Note: Figures in ( ) indicate percentage share of the national total.

Investment within the NET

As noted in table 2.2, in 1992 Hong Kong was by far the largest investor in China, and Taiwan a distant second, with the United States and Japan in third and fourth places. Hong Kong's large share in investment in China conceals its important middleman role. In China's statistics, investment from Hong Kong is not differentiated from investment from subsidiaries of foreign companies incorporated there, which is significant given that multinational companies prefer to test the Chinese market environment through their Hong Kong subsidiaries. Chinese enterprises also invest in China from their Hong Kong subsidiaries to take advantage of the preferences given to foreign investors.

According to preliminary 1993 figures, Hong Kong and Taiwan were the top two investors in China, accounting for respectively 44 and 19 percent of realized FDI in China.[3] The rate of Taiwan's investment, however, increased by 600 percent while

Hong Kong's investment grew at a rate of only 73 percent. If Taiwan further liberalizes its economic interactions with the mainland, it is likely that Taiwanese investment in China will rival that of Hong Kong in the long run because the Taiwanese economy is much bigger than that of Hong Kong.

Hong Kong's Investment in China

Hong Kong's investment in China is extremely diversified, ranging from small-scale, labor-intensive operations to large-scale infrastructure projects. Hong Kong's investment in Guangdong is particularly large. From 1979 to 1993, Guangdong accounted for a third of the cumulative utilized FDI in China, of which 80 percent came from Hong Kong. In turn, of Hong Kong's total FDI in China, 40 percent went to Guangdong.[4]

Hong Kong's industrial investment in Guangdong has transformed Hong Kong manufacturing as well as the entire Hong Kong economy. Currently, Hong Kong manufacturing firms employ up to 3 million workers in Guangdong, while the manufacturing labor force in Hong Kong is only around 650,000. By moving labor-intensive processes to Guangdong, Hong Kong can concentrate on more skill-intensive processes such as product design, sourcing, production management, quality control, and marketing. This arrangement, known as outward processing, has enabled Hong Kong manufacturing to achieve a very high rate of labor productivity growth.

The expansion of exports from processing operations in Guangdong has increased the demand for Hong Kong's service industries, including entrepôt trade, shipping, insurance, business services, and financial services. In fact, both the Hong Kong manufacturing sector and the Hong Kong economy have become increasingly service oriented. In short, Hong Kong has become the economic capital of an industrialized Guangdong.

Before Deng Xiaoping's tour of southern China in early 1992 to encourage economic reforms, the largest corporations in Hong Kong were notably absent from the investment profile in China, which was dominated by small and medium-sized labor-intensive manufacturing firms. Deng's tour stimulated a wave of investment by the major Hong Kong companies, including listed companies such as Cheung Kong, Hutchison-Whampoa, Sun Hung Kai Properties, New World, and Kowloon Wharf, in projects ranging from real estate to infrastructure and commerce. Subsequently, the price of China play shares in the listed companies rose rapidly.[5] In addition, a number of China investment funds were established that invested in industries and B shares in Chinese stock markets. Small investors, besides investing in China play shares and China funds, also purchased presale apartments in Guangdong in droves.

As a result of these developments, Hong Kong's already high share in China's contracted foreign investment rose from 61 percent in 1991 to 69 percent in 1992. This indicates that Hong Kong investors are highly sensitive to investment opportunities in China and were one step ahead of other investors. As other investors jump on the bandwagon of China's boom, Hong Kong's extraordinarily high share will probably decline.

China's Investment in Hong Kong

Hong Kong is the prime destination for China's outward investment. Although precise data are lacking, it appears that China surpassed Japan in 1993 to become the foremost investor in Hong Kong in terms of cumulative investment. According to press reports, the assets owned by Chinese enterprises and government agencies in Hong Kong were $6 billion in 1984 and grew to $10 billion in 1989, doubling to $20 billion in 1992. China's investment in Hong Kong is highly diversified and covers nearly all sectors of the Hong Kong economy, including banking, insurance, entrepôt trade, shipping, aviation, real estate, and manufacturing. China's investment strengthens the ties of Hong Kong to China and enhances Hong Kong's position as the gateway to China.

As China continues to liberalize its foreign exchange controls, it is expected that more and more Chinese capital will flow to Hong Kong through official as well as unofficial channels. It is natural for Chinese enterprises and investors to move their capital to Hong Kong, where property rights are more strictly protected and funds can be used more flexibly. In 1993, partly as the result of the infusion of Chinese capital, real estate prices in Hong Kong soared to record heights, surpassing those in Tokyo.

Although the Chinese yuan is not convertible, the Hong Kong currency has circulated widely (and unofficially) in Guangdong, especially in the Shenzhen SEZ. It has been estimated that the amount of Hong Kong dollars circulating in China amounts to HK$6,300 million (U.S.$808 million), or 16 percent of the total supply of the Hong Kong currency.[6] The gray market for the yuan, which had existed in Hong Kong for some time, reverted to an open market in 1993 when China officially permitted visitors to bring 5,000 yuan into or out of China. Many Hong Kong tourist shops also accept payment in yuan.

Taiwan's Investment in China

Despite the explosive growth of Taiwanese investment on the mainland in recent years, the total stock of contracted Taiwanese investment at the end of 1992 was only 12 percent of that of Hong Kong (table 2.2). This indicates that there is considerable potential for further expansion of the Taiwanese share. Taiwan's investment has largely been in small-scale, labor-intensive operations producing light manufactures for export, including textiles, shoes, umbrellas, travel accessories, and electronics. The projects have been concentrated in Guangdong and particularly in the Xiamen SEZ in Fujian.

Taiwanese investment is increasing in size and sophistication, however, with a growing number of technology-intensive projects such as chemicals, building materials, automobiles, and electronic products and components. The fields of investment have diversified from manufacturing into real estate, finance, tourism, and agriculture and the location of investment has spread inland from the coast.

As noted elsewhere in this volume,[7] the Taiwan government is trying to guide rather than reverse the surge of Taiwanese investment in the mainland, fearing that such investment could lead to the "hollowing out" of Taiwan's industry and to possible security threats. To control the mainland investment boom, for example, both carrots and sticks were used to prevent Formosa Plastics from implementing its gigantic project to build a naphtha cracking plant in Xiamen. Further, although Taiwanese authorities approved a total of 3,319 products for indirect investment in September 1990, they were mostly labor-intensive products with low degrees of processing. Authorization was not granted for investment in industries that were still competitive in Taiwan, including naphtha, catalysts, knitwear, synthetic leather, sheet glass, and glass fibers.

As discussed further in Milton Yeh's chapter, Taiwan has tried to improve the investment environment for Taiwanese investors in the countries of the Association of Southeast Asian Nations (ASEAN). Taiwan is not connected to the mainland by land, as is Hong Kong, so it is no more advantageous for Taiwan to invest in China—ethnic ties in Fujian aside—than in Southeast

Asia; goods have to be loaded from trucks to ships and unloaded again in either case. Hong Kong firms, in contrast, can promptly move parts and components to their mainland subsidiaries by truck and can thus fully exploit the advantage of vertical integration.

The very real political differences dividing the mainland and Taiwan will not disappear overnight. If Taiwan continues to liberalize its relations with the mainland, however, Taiwanese investment in China is likely to rival that of Hong Kong in the long run.

Trade within the NET: Integration of the Commodity Markets

International trade statistics are normally available for countries or customs territories but seldom available for provinces. This section describes trade among China, Hong Kong, and Taiwan instead of trade among Guangdong-Fujian and Taiwan and Hong Kong. As mentioned above, however, some statistics do exist on trade between Guangdong and Hong Kong.

China's Trade with Hong Kong

It is often stated that Hong Kong and China are each other's foremost trading partners, but the statement, although technically true, is misleading because statistics lump together China's trade with third countries via Hong Kong (Hong Kong's entrepôt trade) and China's trade with Hong Kong itself. Because exports are classified by country of destination and imports are classified by country of origin, statistics are further misleading for China's country exports.

For example, in trade between the United States and China, both countries regard their exports to each other through Hong Kong as exports to Hong Kong, thus understating their exports to each other. Imports are not understated because they are traced to the country of origin. Both countries thus overstate their bilateral trade deficits or understate their bilateral surpluses. For example, in 1992, according to U.S. statistics, the United States had a trade deficit of $18 billion with China, whereas China claimed a trade deficit of $306 million with the United States! U.S. statistics are less misleading than those of China, however, because about two-thirds of China's exports to the United States are reexported through Hong Kong, whereas the corresponding percentage for the United States is only about 20 percent.

As a result of pressure from the United States, China has been trying since 1993 to trace the third-country destination of its exports via Hong Kong, and as a result of reclassifying Hong Kong exports as exports to third destinations, China's exports to Hong Kong dropped by 41 percent, and its exports to the United States, Japan, and Germany grew by 97, 35, and 62 percent respectively. Yet this effort at reclassification is incomplete, and it is widely estimated that a substantial portion of China's exports to Hong Kong are still not adequately traced to third countries. This analysis therefore utilizes Hong Kong's rather than China's trade statistics.

Hong Kong's imports of Chinese goods in 1993 totaled $49.8 billion, 94 percent of which were reexported to third countries, only 6 percent being retained in Hong Kong. Although China is by far the foremost supplier of Hong Kong's reexports, representing 58 percent of the total, China's share of Hong Kong's retained imports has stagnated since 1987, falling to 6 percent of the total and behind Japan, the United States, and Taiwan. This is because China has been unable to capture the higher end of Hong Kong's market, which is dominated by Japan. Given the increasing affluence of Hong Kong and the Japanese dominance in vehicles, capital goods, and quality consumer durable and consumer goods, the future of Chinese products in Hong Kong is not very bright.

Hong Kong was the largest final market (excluding Chinese exports via Hong Kong) for Chinese exports in the late 1960s and early 1970s, when Japan and the United States began to dominate. China continued to regard Hong Kong as its largest market until 1992, when it began reclassifying exports destined for third countries. As a result, in 1993, Hong Kong's imports from China accounted for 54 percent of China's total exports, 51 percent of which were reexports and only 3.3 percent being retained in Hong Kong.

Hong Kong's 1993 exports to China totaled $43.3 billion, 81 percent of which were reexports of third-country goods to China and 19 percent, or $8.1 billion, of which were Hong Kong's domestic exports to China. The latter category has grown rapidly from negligible amounts, largely owing to Hong Kong investment in processing/assembling operations in China. Hong Kong firms supply such operations with the required raw materials and components, parts of which are made in Hong Kong. In

1993, China surpassed the United States to become the foremost market for Hong Kong products, taking 28 percent of Hong Kong's domestic exports.

Although China was the largest market for Hong Kong products, Hong Kong was only the fourth largest supplier to China after Japan, the United States, and Taiwan. In 1993, the shares of Taiwan and Hong Kong in China's imports were 13 percent and 8 percent, respectively. It should be noted that China regarded Hong Kong as its largest supplier from 1987 till 1992, when Chinese trade statistics began to trace incoming exports from third countries via Hong Kong. In 1993, Hong Kong reexports to China accounted for 34 percent of China's imports. Hong Kong's total exports (including both reexports and domestic exports) thus accounted for 42 percent of China's imports in 1993.

Both outward processing and the decentralization of China's foreign trade have boosted Hong Kong's trade with China, both in its reexports of Chinese goods to third countries and its reexports of third-country goods to China. Decentralization has vastly increased the number of trading partners for China and raised the cost of searching for suitable partners. Intermediation has emerged to economize on search costs, and this demand for intermediation has been channeled to Hong Kong due to its efficiency in trading.

The importance of outward processing for the Hong Kong and southern Chinese economies—and of Hong Kong's entrepôt trade more generally—is borne out by the statistics: outward processing and entrepôt trade together accounted for 74 percent of Hong Kong's domestic exports to China, 46 percent of Hong Kong's reexports to China, and 72 percent of Hong Kong's imports from China. In 1979, when economic reforms began, China's goods reexported via Hong Kong accounted for only 7 percent of China's total exports, rising to 51 percent in 1993. Reexport of third-country goods to China via Hong Kong was only 2 percent of China's imports in 1979, rising to 34 percent in 1993.

Guangdong's Trade with Hong Kong

Guangdong's trade with Hong Kong is significant and accounts for the bulk of Guangdong's trade as well as of Hong Kong's trade with China. In 1992, Hong Kong's imports from Guangdong related to outward processing were $30.6 billion. Besides exports from processing operations, Guangdong's exports from "general trade" were $9.2 billion, of which at least 80 percent (or $7.4 billion) were exports to Hong Kong. Hong Kong's total imports from Guangdong in 1992 are thus at least $37.9 billion, making up 86 percent of Hong Kong's imports from China.

In 1992, Guangdong accounted for 93 percent of Hong Kong's imports related to outward processing ($32.8 billion) and accounted for at least 64 percent of Hong Kong's other imports from China ($11.4 billion). Hong Kong's 1992 exports to China related to outward processing were $18.3 billion, and around 93 percent of this was destined for Guangdong, because it accounted for 93 percent of Hong Kong's imports related to outward processing in China. This gives a figure of $17 billion for Hong Kong's exports to Guangdong related to outward processing. In addition, there is a substantial amount of trade not related to outward processing. It is safe to conclude, then, that in 1992 Hong Kong's exports to Guangdong accounted for the bulk of Guangdong's imports of $32.3 billion as well as Hong Kong's exports to China of $35.4 billion.

In China's trade with its major partners (including the United States, Canada, Japan, Singapore, Germany, the United Kingdom, Australia, France, and Italy), the effect of China's trade decentralization has overwhelmed the decrease in the costs of establishing direct trade links, and China relies more and more on indirect trade via Hong Kong.[8]

China's Service Trade with Hong Kong

Trade in services between the mainland and Hong Kong is extremely important. Conceptually, the reexport margin that Hong Kong earns through entrepôt trade in fact represents export of services. Such services are embodied in the goods sold, however, and are normally recorded in trade statistics as export of goods rather than export of services. Reliable data are therefore lacking for critical services provided in such fields as transportation, trading, construction, finance, and business consulting. According to one source, half of the foreign law firms in Hong Kong provide legal advice on China's trade.[9]

As the foremost gateway for foreigners entering China, Hong Kong keeps statistics for tourist services. Visitors to Hong Kong accounted for roughly two-thirds of China's tourist arrivals as well as expenditures in the early 1990s. Although China has increased its direct air links with other countries since 1979, the percentage of foreign tourists arriving and leaving China via Hong Kong has grown since 1982, rising to 55 and 44 percent, respectively, in 1987. This paradox is explained by China's decentralization of authorized, organized tours from the China Travel Service to provincial and local authorities in the early 1980s. This decentralization increases search costs and the demand for intermediation, in which Hong Kong excels. In addition, Taiwan's removal of its ban on travel to the mainland in 1987 led to another jump in the number of foreigners visiting China via Hong Kong.

Hong Kong also provides crucial services as an entrepôt and transshipment center for China. It is estimated that in 1990, Hong Kong's transshipment of goods to and from China via Hong Kong amounted to 4 and 6 percent of China's imports and exports by value. Hong Kong trading firms also perform a valuable brokerage role for China's direct trade, which is to roughly 7 percent of China's overall trade.[10] In the absence of more recent data, we can apply the 1990 shares to 1993. The shares of China's exports consumed, reexported, transshipped, and intermediated by Hong Kong in 1993 would then be 3, 51, 6, and 7 percent, respectively, totaling 67 percent. On the import side, the shares of China's imports produced, reexported, transshipped, and intermediated by Hong Kong in 1993 were 8, 34, 4, and 7 percent, respectively, totaling 53 percent. Hong Kong thus plays an important role in two-thirds of China's exports and in more than half of China's imports.

China's exports of services to Hong Kong have also increased rapidly in recent years. Chinese construction firms are active in projects in Hong Kong, and many mainland Chinese work in Hong Kong, including manufacturing workers imported to relieve the labor shortage and engineers working in mainland-owned factories. The Hong Kong populace also travels to China for medical treatment because the cost is dramatically lower there.

China's Trade with Taiwan

The explosive growth of Taiwan's trade with the mainland in the form of Hong Kong reexports is well known and regularly reported. Hong Kong statistics on its reexports of Taiwanese origin to the mainland and of mainland origin to Taiwan have often been used by researchers to gauge the magnitude of Taiwan-mainland trade. What is not well known is that despite the official ban on direct trade, there is, in fact, substantial "direct" trade between Taiwan and the mainland.

This "direct" trade usually involves the switching of trade documents. Taiwanese exporters claim that their goods are destined for Hong Kong when the goods leave Taiwan; however, on arrival in Hong Kong, the trade documents are switched, and now claim that the goods are destined for the mainland. Because the goods are consigned to a buyer on the mainland, they do not go through Hong Kong customs and no Hong Kong firm claims legal possession of the goods. Such goods are regarded as transshipment or "cargo in transit" by the Hong Kong government and are not regarded as part of Hong Kong's trade. Such trade is called "direct" trade in this analysis because it looks like indirect trade in terms of trade documentation, involving two separate sets of trade documents, but it is direct trade in reality because no third party buys the goods involved for resale. By switching trade documents, Taiwanese exporters save on the cost of Hong Kong customs fees and taxes, which are actually quite minor, amounting to only 0.1 percent of the value of goods traded. This "direct" trade also has the advantage of confidentiality because Hong Kong customs has no records of the trade, and it is very difficult for anyone to find out who has sold what to whom.

This "direct" trade has three distinct modalities—transshipment, transit shipment, and illegal direct shipment. *Transshipment* involves the uploading and downloading of cargo from one vessel to another, usually in Hong Kong waters. Because Taiwan does not permit cargo to be carried between Taiwan and the mainland in the same vessel, and there is no regular shipping between Taiwan and the mainland, transshipment is the dominant mode of "direct" trade. The Hong Kong government maintains statistics on the volume of transshipment by weight but not by value, because transshipped goods do not clear Hong Kong customs.

Transit shipment refers to a process whereby ships stop in Hong Kong waters on their way to or from the mainland, and do not transship their cargoes, which proceed in the same vessel. This practice developed from the October 1988 Taiwanese law allowing chartered ships and airplanes flying the flags of third countries to sail or fly between Taiwan and the mainland as long as they stopped in a third place in the voyage and their cargo or passengers did not continue in the same vessel or plane. Yet because in practice it is difficult for Taiwanese authorities to verify whether cargo has changed vessels or not, Taiwanese-chartered ships generally merely stop in Hong Kong waters, where their contents are treated by the Hong Kong government as "cargo in transit," and then continue the journey without transshipping their cargoes. This practice offers considerable cost and time savings as no downloading and uploading are involved.[11] The Hong Kong government does not keep statistics on cargo in transit.

It is known from press reports and interviews that *illegal direct shipment* involving chartered ships flying flags of third countries may be common. Although illegal direct shipment obviously saves transportation costs, it is risky because shipping records are public information and the Taiwan government can check if the ship has passed through Hong Kong or a third port. Ships have been fined for illegal direct shipment.[12]

In the above three forms of "direct" trade, Taiwan usually records the exports as destined for Hong Kong even though the goods are not recorded as imports to Hong Kong and are shipped on to the mainland. Thus, Taiwan's "direct" exports to the mainland should be equal to the difference between Taiwan's exports to Hong Kong and Hong Kong's imports from Taiwan, after adjusting for the cost of insurance and freight (or the c.i.f. and f.o.b. prices). This represents an application of the trade-partners statistics technique.

Table 2.3 shows an estimation of the value of Taiwan's "direct" trade with the mainland. From 1975 to 1987, before Taiwan's liberalization of its mainland policy, Hong Kong's imports from Taiwan were 5 percent larger than Taiwan's exports to Hong Kong; the difference represents insurance and freight costs because "direct" trade was nearly nonexistent before the 1987 liberalization. Since 1988, however, Taiwan's exports to Hong Kong have exceeded Hong Kong's imports from Taiwan by an increasingly huge margin.

Table 2.4 shows Taiwan's "direct" and indirect trade with China. In 1993, Taiwan's "direct" exports to the mainland were $6,973 million, exceeding Taiwan's indirect exports to the mainland via Hong Kong of $6,266 million. Taiwan's 1993 exports to the mainland via Hong Kong (including direct and indirect exports) were thus $13,239 million, making up 16 percent of Taiwan's total exports.

Unlike the case of exports, Taiwan's imports from the mainland are restricted to selected commodity categories, and prohibited goods from the mainland are imported into Taiwan with fake country-of-origin certificates. For example, a Thai certificate

Table 2.3
Taiwan's Exports to Hong Kong and China, 1988–1993
(in millions of U.S. dollars)

		Taiwan's Exports to Hong Kong					China's Imports from Taiwan
	Total	Imported into Hong Kong				"Direct exports" to China	
		Subtotal	Retained for internal use	Reexported			
				to China	elsewhere		
1988	5580	5344	3209	1964	171	236	–
	(100)	(95.8)	(57.5)	(35.2)	(3.1)	(4.2)	
1989	7030	6237	3376	2540	321	793	1856
	(100)	(88.7)	(48.0)	(36.1)	(4.6)	(11.3)	
1990	8570	7045	3832	2875	338	1525	2254
	(100)	(82.2)	(44.7)	(33.5)	(3.9)	(17.8)	
1991	12418	9019	4354	4074	591	3399	3639
	(100)	(72.6)	(35.1)	(32.8)	(4.8)	(27.4)	
1992	15427	10722	4607	5509	606	4705	5881
	(100)	(69.5)	(29.9)	(35.7)	(3.9)	(30.5)	
1993	18455	11482	4275	6596	611	6973	12933
	(100)	(62.2)	(23.2)	(35.7)	(3.3)	(37.8)	

Sources: Taiwan's exports to Hong Kong are obtained from the *Monthly Statistics of the Republic of China*.
   The amounts imported into Hong Kong are taken to be Hong Kong's imports from Taiwan (obtained from *Hong Kong Review of Overseas Trade*) less a 5 percent margin to allow for the cost of freight and insurance.
   Taiwan's exports reexported via Hong Kong to China and elsewhere are taken to be Hong Kong's reexport of Taiwanese goods to China and elsewhere (obtained from *Hong Kong Review of Overseas Trade*) less a 15 percent reexport markup.
   Taiwan's reexport[s] retained for internal use in Hong Kong are obtained as a residual.
   "Direct exports" to China are obtained as a residual.
   China's imports from Taiwan are obtained from China customs statistics.

Note: Figures in ( ) represent the percentage distribution of Taiwan's exports to Hong Kong.

of origin can be obtained for a mere $100.[13] Given this procedure, it is not possible to estimate Taiwan's "direct" imports from the mainland as the difference between Taiwan's imports from Hong Kong and Hong Kong's exports to Taiwan, because the imports are recorded from the country appearing on the fake country-of-

Table 2.4
Taiwan's "Direct" and Indirect Trade with China, 1986–1993

	Exports (U.S. $ millions)			Imports (U.S. $ millions)			Transshipment via Hong Kong (tons)	
	"Direct"	Indirect[a]	Total	"Direct"	Indirect[b]	Total	To China	From China
1986	23	670	693	0	151	151	1,300	800
1987	92	908	1,000	17	303	320	500	900
1988	236	1,866	2,102	14	502	516	7,549	2,595
1989	793	2,413	3,206	37	616	653	33,283	6,662
1990	1,525	2,731	4,256	70	804	874	43,757	12,447
1991	3,399	3,870	7,269	501	1,187	1,688	272,475	87,610
1992	4,705	5,233	9,938	1,219	1,184	2,403	527,427	211,026
1993	6,973	6,266	13,239	–	1,159	–	–	–

[a] Taiwan's indirect exports are taken to be Hong Kong's reexports to China of Taiwan origin less a 15 percent reexport markup and then less a 5 percent margin to allow for the cost of insurance and freight.

[b] Taiwan's indirect imports are taken to be Hong Kong's reexports to Taiwan of China origin plus a 5 percent margin to allow for the cost of insurance and freight.

origin certificate. Therefore, Taiwan's "direct" imports from the mainland are estimated from the weight of Hong Kong's transshipment of mainland goods to Taiwan and an estimate of the value per ton of such transshipment across different commodity categories (table 2.4).[14] This gives a 1992 estimate of $1,219 million, exceeding the value of Hong Kong's reexports of mainland goods to Taiwan by 8 percent. Since 1992, Hong Kong's reexports of mainland goods to Taiwan have stagnated while transshipment of mainland goods to Taiwan has continued to soar (table 2.3). Thus, there is evidently a substitution of "direct" for indirect trade.

Taiwan has a massive surplus in its commodity trade with the mainland, partly because of Taiwan's policy of importing selected items only and partly because of the lack of mainland competitiveness in producing goods demanded in Taiwan.

Taiwan has, however, large deficits with the mainland in tourism, gifts and remittances, and investment, so that the balance of payments across the Taiwan Strait is actually more even. Moreover, intraindustry trade is expected to develop rapidly with the surge of Taiwanese investment on the mainland and the further liberalization of Taiwan's controls on imports from the mainland.

Based on this analysis, trade between Taiwan and the mainland has grown extremely fast and is now very substantial. In 1992, Taiwan's total exports to the mainland via Hong Kong were $9,938 million, or 12.3 percent of Taiwan's exports. After adjusting for Hong Kong's reexport margin and the cost of insurance and freight, the mainland's total imports from Taiwan are $11,551 million, or 14.3 percent of the mainland's total imports. In 1992, the mainland surpassed Japan to become the second largest market for Taiwan after the United States, which has a market share of 28.9 percent. From 1979 to 1992, Taiwan's exports to the mainland increased 393 times, and the average annual rate of growth was 58 percent. Taiwan's exports to the United States have declined in absolute terms since 1987, and the mainland may become Taiwan's largest market in a few years' time.

By 1991, the mainland's imports from Taiwan constituted 13 percent of its total imports, and Taiwan had surpassed Hong Kong and the United States to become the mainland's second-largest supplier after Japan, which has a share of 20 percent. If present trends continue, Taiwan will soon become the mainland's largest supplier.

Taiwan's imports from the mainland are smaller, for the reasons given above of selective importation and China's lack of competitive advantage. In 1992, Taiwan's total imports from the mainland via Hong Kong were $2,403 million, or 3.3 percent of the total. After adjusting for Hong Kong's reexport margin and the cost of insurance and freight, total mainland exports to Taiwan were $2,100 million, or 2.5 percent of its total exports. In 1992, the mainland became the fourth-largest supplier to Taiwan after Japan (30.2 percent), the United States (21.9 percent), and Germany (5.4 percent), just surpassing South Korea (3.2 percent). Taiwan has also become a significant market for the mainland. From 1983 to 1992, Taiwan's total imports from the mainland via Hong Kong increased 23 times and the average annual rate of growth was 43 percent. Given this rate of growth, Taiwan's imports from the mainland will soon be very significant.

Service trade between the mainland and Taiwan is largely restricted to visits by Taiwanese tourists to China. After Hong Kong and Macao, Taiwan is the third highest source of tourists for the mainland, accounting for 4 percent of tourist arrivals in China in 1993. Taiwan's share of tourist expenditure in China is likely to be a few times higher than its share in tourist arrivals because Taiwanese visitors spend more on a per capita basis than the short-term visitors from Hong Kong and Macao. Most of the Taiwanese visiting China do so via Hong Kong. In recent years, Taiwan has been the number one source of tourists for Hong Kong, accounting for 20 percent of tourist arrivals in 1993. Of the 1.75 million Taiwanese tourists who visited Hong Kong that year, 1.5 million went to the mainland.[15]

Trade and Investment between Hong Kong and Taiwan

Prior to 1987, economic ties between Hong Kong and Taiwan were one-sided due to Taiwan's trade protectionism and foreign exchange controls. In the mid-1970s, Hong Kong became Taiwan's third-largest market after the United States and Japan, accounting for roughly 7 percent of Taiwan's exports. The barriers against Hong Kong goods in Taiwan were, however, quite high. Hong Kong was the third-largest investor in Taiwan after the United States and Japan, but Taiwanese investment in Hong Kong was insignificant owing to Taiwan's then-stringent foreign exchange controls.

In the late 1980s, however, economic ties between Hong Kong and Taiwan developed extremely rapidly with the liberalization of Taiwan's imports and foreign exchange controls, the sharp appreciation of the Taiwanese currency, and Taiwan's use of Hong Kong as an intermediary in its interactions with the mainland. By the end of 1989, Hong Kong investment in Taiwan totaled $1.2 billion, or 11 percent of total inward investment in Taiwan, while investments from Japan and the United States were $3 billion and $2.9 billion, respectively. Taiwan's investment in Hong Kong also soared. Cumulative investment from Taiwan reached $2 billion by the end of 1989, half of which was invested after 1987. Taiwan became the fifth-largest investor in Hong Kong after the mainland, Japan, the United States, and the United Kingdom.

As can be seen from table 2.3, Hong Kong is an important final market (excluding Taiwanese goods reexported via Hong Kong) for Taiwan. In 1992, Hong Kong's retained imports from

Taiwan were $4,607 million, or 9.2 percent of Hong Kong's total retained imports. Taiwan is the third-largest supplier of Hong Kong's retained imports after Japan and the United States. After adjusting for the cost of insurance and freight, Taiwan's 1992 exports for final use in Hong Kong were $4,388 million, or 5.4 percent of Taiwan's total exports. Hong Kong was the fourth-largest final market for Taiwan after the United States (28.9 percent), the mainland (12.3 percent), and Japan (10.9 percent). The share of Hong Kong as a final market for Taiwan has declined slightly in the early 1990s due to the surge of Taiwan's exports to the mainland. The share of the Taiwan market in Hong Kong's domestic exports jumped from 1 percent in 1985 to 2.7 percent in 1993, amounting to $803 million. Since 1986, Taiwan has been the seventh-largest market for Hong Kong after the United States, China, Germany, the United Kingdom, Japan, and Singapore.

Integration of the Labor Market in the NET

There are fundamental reasons for the lack of integration in the labor market among the NET entities. The mainland has few controls to prevent Hong Kong and Taiwan residents from working on the mainland, so that in the early 1990s, some 45,000 to 55,000 Hong Kong residents have reported that they had worked in China, according to Census and Statistics Department surveys. Controls against visitors from the mainland in Hong Kong and particularly Taiwan, however, are very restrictive, although illegal migrants from the mainland are not uncommon in both places, given their tight labor markets.

China and Hong Kong have agreed to a quota restricting the number of immigrants from China to no more than 75 per day or 27,375 per year. This means that the mainland relatives of Hong Kong residents have to wait a long time before they can migrate to Hong Kong; even spouses normally have to wait for 10 years.

Although the Hong Kong barrier against permanent migration from the mainland is high, limitations for temporary stays have been reduced in recent years. Since 1989, when the Hong Kong government embarked on the first labor-importation scheme, more and more Chinese workers have come to Hong Kong to work on temporary contracts. The third labor-importation scheme, announced in January of 1992, further doubled the labor intake quota to 25,000, practically all of whom will be workers from China.

Recently, the barriers for professional workers from China have also been relaxed, and these workers are eligible to become permanent residents of Hong Kong. Since 1990, Hong Kong employers have been permitted to employ mainland professionals who have stayed overseas for more than two years. In April 1994, the Hong Kong government announced a trial scheme to import 1,000 mainland graduates.

There are few restrictions against mainlanders entering Hong Kong on official passports, and it is estimated that more than 60,000 are working in mainland companies in Hong Kong. Given Hong Kong's tight labor market, a substantial but unknown number of illegal immigrants as well as legal short-term visitors participate illegally in the labor market.

In just a few years, tourists from the mainland have increased from a trickle to more than 1.5 million in 1993, and the mainland is behind only Taiwan as a source of tourists. Given present rates of growth, the mainland was expected to surpass Taiwan in this area in 1994.

The Basic Law—the future constitution of Hong Kong after its reversion to China—stipulates that direct relatives of Hong Kong residents have the right to enter Hong Kong. There are currently about 200,000 direct relatives of Hong Kong residents on the mainland who have not yet migrated. This number will grow because Hong Kong-mainland marriages are increasingly common. By 1997, or even before then, the present strict controls against immigration from the mainland will have to be relaxed.

Future Prospects for Economic Integration within the NET

Economic forces point to a rapid continuation of economic integration within the NET. Yet whether China can preserve law and order in the post-Deng era is uncertain, and the stability of Hong Kong—the pivot of the NET's economic integration—is not assured. If China manages to maintain stability and continue its pragmatic policy of opening and reform in the post-Deng era, then it is safe to assume that Hong Kong will be stable and the NET will continue to prosper. Investors appear to be very bullish over the future of Hong Kong and have discounted the breakdown in Sino-British negotiations over the electoral reforms of Hong Kong's Legislative Council in the transition to 1997. Their investments have sent the prices of

Hong Kong's real estate market and stock market to record heights. The emigration of Hong Kong's professionals has slowed down, and there has been a marked increase in returning migrants.

Prospects for Processing Operations

The rise of wages and land prices in Guangdong and increasing world protectionism have sparked a concern that the outward-oriented, labor-intensive processing operations in Guangdong and Fujian have no future. This concern is premature. Although wages have risen rapidly in Guangdong, the yuan has also depreciated rapidly, and wages have also risen rapidly in Hong Kong and Taiwan, so that the gap in wages between Hong Kong and Guangdong has not in fact shrunk. Although land prices have sharply risen in Shenzhen and other SEZs, there are vast areas near Hong Kong where land is still cheap. Because Guangdong and Fujian have a combined population of nearly 100 million, and the supply of out-of-province labor is more or less unlimited, the primary supply bottlenecks are lack of roads, ports, power, and infrastructure, rather than the availability of cheap labor and land.

Protectionism is certainly a problem. China's most favored nation (MFN) status with the United States has been the subject of debates about its renewal every year, and although now not formally linked to human rights issues, its revocation may come under other pressures in future years. China is running up against its quota of textiles and clothing exports, and the number of antidumping charges against it is increasing fast. The problem on the demand side is exaggerated, however. Although China's exports to the United States have rapidly increased, Hong Kong and Taiwan exports to the United States have declined as a result of the relocation of their industries to China. Combined U.S. exports to the NET entities have also grown dramatically because of their increasing economic prosperity and trade liberalization policies. In fact, the absolute size of the U.S. trade deficit with the NET entities combined has been roughly constant since 1987, and its size relative to U.S. exports has shrunk markedly.

Although China is approaching its quota constraints in its clothing exports, the possibility of quality upgrading should not be ignored. Thanks to quality upgrading, China's clothing exports registered a healthy growth of 9.3 percent in 1993 despite restrictions. Moreover, China has a large import market and thereby has considerable bargaining power in world trade. The decision of the Clinton administration over China's MFN status shows that even the United States has to reckon with China's power in world trade.

The growth rates of Hong Kong's imports from China related to outward processing are good indicators of the performance of outward processing operations in the NET, which grew 28 percent in 1990, 36 percent in 1991, 29 percent in 1992, and 17 percent for the first three quarters of 1993. Despite recent decelerated growth, the rates are still very high, showing that there is still appreciable potential for the further development of processing operations.

The Opening of China's Domestic Market to Foreign Investment

Since Deng's southern tour in early 1992, China has relaxed its strict controls on allowing joint ventures to sell products in the domestic market, which has led to high expectations on the part of foreign investors. Foreign investors aiming at China's domestic market cannot, however, recoup their capital unless China makes the yuan more convertible. Although China is taking steps to facilitate convertibility, the yuan is vulnerable to rapid depreciation due to the tremendous inflationary pressures in China, and taming this inflation, in turn, is key to further liberalization of exchange controls. Convertibility thus depends on these critical and interlocking factors, and foreign investment aimed at the domestic market will be limited until the problems they raised are resolved. Experience illustrates that the reform of financial systems in Communist or former Communist countries is an arduous process, and foreign investors should be cautioned against the rosy expectations conjured up by a market of 1.2 billion people.

Furthermore, allowing foreign-invested enterprises to sell in the domestic market can be detrimental to China unless it liberalizes import controls to allow the direct importation of foreign goods. The inflow of foreign capital in highly protected industries is likely to result in immiserizing foreign investment. This occurs because protected industries normally do not have a comparative advantage, and their protection results in a misallocation of resources: Too many resources are drawn into the production of the protected, import-substituting good, and, as a result, too few resources are devoted to the production of the exportable good. Allowing inflows of foreign capital into the protected industry will lead to a further expansion of that industry and, consequently, greater misallocation of resources, reducing the country's gross national product (GNP) and overall welfare.

China generally prohibits foreign investors from selling in the domestic market, which is a commendable policy because it avoids the pitfall of immiserizing foreign investment. China has, however, been making special exemptions, usually with the rationale of "exchanging markets for technology." Comparative advantage determines whether this rationale would be beneficial to China. If China has a potential comparative advantage in producing a certain good but that potential is not realized for lack of know-how, "exchanging markets for technology" can be beneficial. China can use temporary protection to attract foreign investment in order to acquire the know-how and can then realize the comparative advantage, after which protection is no longer necessary. Yet if a good needs permanent protection to be profitable, it must be because China does not have a comparative advantage in the production of that good and acquiring the know-how is not worthwhile. Attracting technology for products in which China does not have a comparative advantage only leads to the growth of inappropriate and inefficient industries. Under such circumstances, an increase in foreign capital inflow will lead to a fall in China's economic welfare and GNP.

As China increasingly allows foreign investors to sell domestically, import liberalization will become an urgent problem. With import liberalization, foreign-invested enterprises have to face international prices and the pressures of international competition. The pitfalls of immiserizing foreign investment can thereby be avoided.

Prospect of Direct Links between Taiwan and the Mainland

The prospect of Taiwan-mainland trade is undoubtedly bright because the two economies are complementary as well as dynamic. Taiwan has made it clear that it will not permit direct economic links with the mainland unless Beijing renounces the use of force over the Taiwan Strait, an option that Beijing is so far unwilling to give up. A breakthrough cannot be ruled out in the post-Deng era, however.

Although the prohibition of direct economic links between China and Taiwan is quite costly to Taiwan, it is estimated that Hong Kong would lose as much as $1 billion from the opening of such links owing to losses in transportation, trade, telecommunications, and tourism. The gain for Taiwan would probably be even greater because direct links save transportation time and open up many new economic opportunities.

The impact of the official opening of direct trade between the two economies, however, may not be as dramatic as expected because, as noted above, half of the existing trade is already "direct." In addition, Taiwan has increasingly softened the interpretation of its ban on direct trade, decreasing the cost of "direct" trade and most likely leading to the substitution of "direct" for indirect trade. On the other hand, the mainland has continued to decentralize its trading system, which has led to an increase in search costs and in reliance on intermediation, particularly the extensive trading networks of Hong Kong.

Taiwan-mainland trade provides an interesting case for studying the impact of direct trade on indirect trade because the relative advantage of direct to indirect trade is particularly significant for Taiwan. The savings in transportation costs of direct trade are large because Taiwan is close to the mainland. Moreover, the search cost of direct trade is comparatively low for Taiwan because of cultural proximity. Taiwanese firms also have large trading networks on the mainland. Around half of Taiwan-mainland trade, however, is still taking the form of indirect trade via Hong Kong despite the availability of "direct" trade. This confirms the efficiency of Hong Kong in intermediation. Although direct trade between China and South Korea was recently opened, a substantial portion of this trade continues to go through Hong Kong.[16] The opening of direct Taiwan-mainland trade may have the same outcome.

Even if Taiwan decides to initiate direct links today, the negotiation of direct air or sea links is often time-consuming in the best of circumstances. With political mistrust on both sides, the negotiations will probably be protracted, so that the impact of direct Taiwan-mainland trade is likely to be gradual.

Prospect of Further Integration

Because of the many differences in the political, legal, and economic systems of the mainland on the one hand and "maritime

China" (Hong Kong and Taiwan) on the other, economic integration of the mainland with maritime China will be highly uneven. Integration will proceed rapidly in some areas but slowly in others. Between the mainland and maritime China, controls on movements of goods are relatively liberal, whereas controls on capital and foreign exchange are more strict, and controls on migration are strictest of all. Integration of the commodity markets will proceed rapidly due to the relatively mild controls on the flow of goods. It is important to distinguish, however, between export-processing and import-competing industries. The outward-processing operations of maritime China on the mainland have developed extremely rapidly because their products are exported and they are not hampered by China's foreign exchange controls. The growth of external investment in China's import-competing industries will necessarily be slower due to the same controls.

The integration of service industries between the mainland and maritime China will similarly be slow because most services cannot be exported and are sold in the domestic market. Moreover, providing services requires people-to-people contacts, and the controls of maritime China on migration from the mainland will hamper the full integration of services.

The integration of the financial markets between the mainland and maritime China will also be quite slow because China's foreign exchange controls on the capital account are likely to be quite strict even in the medium term. The integration of the labor markets between the mainland and maritime China will probably be very slow because of controls on migration.

Although integration in these sectors will be slow, overall the huge investments among the trio imply that the interests of southern China, Hong Kong, and Taiwan are tied together. For instance, if the United States were to revoke China's MFN status, all entities in the NET would lose heavily. Similarly, the three parties would gain if China and Taiwan were to gain entry into the new World Trade Organization.

Notes

1. The economy of Macao can be regarded as an appendage of Hong Kong and will not be treated separately here.

2. Sung Yun-wing, "Non-Institutional Economic Integration via Cultural Affinity: The Case of China, Taiwan, and Hong Kong," occasional

paper no. 13 (Hong Kong Institute of Asia-Pacific Studies, Chinese University of Hong Kong, July 1992), 8.

3. *Economic Daily*, January 17, 1994.

4. As a further measure of Guangdong's capital inflow, it is useful to note that inward FDI in China in 1992 was $11 billion, of which $3.6 billion went to Guangdong, while Thailand's inward FDI was $2.1 billion. In fact, the investment boom in China and Guangdong has appeared to have affected inward FDI in Southeast Asia adversely.

5. "China play shares" are shares in companies that are registered outside of China but that do a majority of their business in China.

6. *Hong Kong Economic Times*, March 21, 1991.

7. See chapter 5.

8. Sung Yun-wing, *The China-Hong Kong Connection: The Key to China's Open Door Policy* (Cambridge: Cambridge University Press, 1991), 141–143.

9. *Intertrade*, October 1984, p. 2.

10. Sung, "Non-Institutional Economic Integration," 19.

11. Sung Yun-wing, "The Economics of the Illegal Trade between Taiwan and Mainland China" (paper presented to the International Pacific Rim Conference of the Western Economic Association, Hong Kong, January 8–13, 1994), 13.

12. Ibid., 14.

13. Ibid., 19.

14. The value of Taiwan's "direct" imports (estimated by the trade-partners statistics technique) in the pre-liberalization era of 1983 to 1987 was divided by the weight of Hong Kong's transshipment of mainland goods to Taiwan. In the pre-liberalization era, the use of fake certificates of origin was rare. The estimation appears to be quite robust because it gives results similar to those in another method of estimation (Ibid., 20).

15. *Hong Kong Economic Journal*, April 13, 1994.

16. Sung, "Economics of Illegal Trade," 22.

3

Return of the Prodigals:
The Overseas Chinese and
Southern China's Economic Boom

Sally Stewart

This chapter evaluates a cultural thread common to the overseas Chinese based in Hong Kong, Taiwan, Singapore, Malaysia, Indonesia, and Thailand and considers their central
contribution to the prosperity of the coastal belt of the People's
Republic of China from which most of them originated.

The southern China natural economic territory (NET) epito-
mizes the complex contribution overseas Chinese make to
China's dynamic economic growth because it embraces the area
that was once their ancestral home.[1] It is a totally informal economic region that, without any legal framework or political and
bureaucratic intervention, transcends national boundaries to
constitute the fastest-growing economy in the world. This
region—defined in this analysis as the coastal belt from the
Yangtze delta to the Pearl River delta, and including Hong Kong
and Taiwan—contains about 250 million people and embraces
four different political and economic systems: Chinese socialist,
British colonial, Taiwanese capitalist, and Portuguese colonial.
The officials of these areas have never met to discuss the growth
of the NET, and they have designed no specific measures to
reduce customs barriers or to harmonize trade policies. Yet the
entrepreneurs of these varied territories have collaborated to the
huge mutual benefit of all the component entities.

My central thesis is that this economic phenomenon owes a
great deal to the investment, marketing, and management skills
of the overseas Chinese, and their presence explains why economic development occurred first in the south rather than, for
instance, around Shanghai, which was the traditional economic
powerhouse of China. In Milton Friedman's words, "The overseas Chinese have so far been a large part of the dynamic driving
force which is promoting Chinese development."[2]

Who Are the "Overseas Chinese"?

By *overseas Chinese* is meant here those ethnic Chinese who, themselves or their ancestors, have settled outside China's borders. At one end of the spectrum are those who have lived overseas for centuries, learning the local tongue at the expense of the Chinese language while retaining Chinese social customs, such as the Babas of Malaysia. At the other end of the spectrum are the Chinese communities in such Western countries as Canada and Australia, many of whom are far from integrated into the society of their new home. For the sake of simplicity, the "compatriots"—to use Beijing's phrase for those from Hong Kong, Taiwan, and Macao—are also included.

These estimated 55 million ethnic Chinese living outside China, with their marked entrepreneurial tendencies and business networks, have been a major factor in the economic growth of Southeast Asia and southern China over the last decade.[3]

Factors in the East Asian Success Stories

The debate in scholarly circles over the various factors responsible for the success of East Asian economies is quite extensive. It has been suggested that the development model that best fits these states, as well as China, is the Bureaucratic Authoritarian Industrializing Regime paradigm, which argues that government has been the prime facilitator of economic dynamism.[4] A 1993 International Finance Corporation discussion paper also strongly supports the view that active government intervention contributed greatly to the economic success of South Korea, Taiwan, and Singapore and played a major role in boosting private investment.[5] Scholars have also cited the importance of institutional factors and of "public administrations of the competence and integrity that characterize these East Asian countries" as prime reasons for economic success.[6]

Yet the Confucian element is also of significance in these countries; the Sinic (Chinese) and "Vulgar" Confucian influences—in contrast to the classical Confucian model—have been widely canvassed in academic circles as a prime cause of their economic success.[7] Regarding Taiwan, although several scholars give more weight to governmental influence than to the Confucian heritage, the similarities between "Victorian virtues" (to use Margaret Thatcher's phrase) and the values inculcated by

Figure 3.1
Little Dragons: A Model showing Major Common Factors in the
Development of the High-Performing Asian Economies

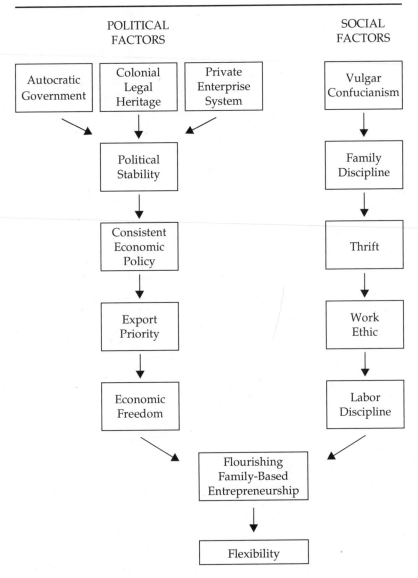

Sources: S. G. Redding, *The Spirit of Chinese Capitalism* (New York: Walter de Gruyter, 1990), and Edward K. Y. Chen, *Hyper-Growth in Asian Economies* (London: Macmillan, 1979).

"Vulgar" Confucianism tend to support the thesis—first advanced by Max Weber in 1930—that a group's long-term view and willingness to save are of crucial importance to ensuring its economic well-being.[8]

In the business area, the overseas Chinese often follow this strategy of being content with low profits while building up market share. Yet some studies suggest that their success is largely due to their being hardy, self-reliant, and, above all, willing to take risks.[9] Still other scholars assert that Confucian values, such as thrift and perseverance, are vital for entrepreneurial success and stress the importance of the long-term versus short-term orientation that is found in Hong Kong, Taiwan, Japan, South Korea, and Singapore.[10]

Whatever weight is given to these various factors, the significance of the overseas Chinese presence seems difficult to deny. According to the *Far Eastern Economic Review*, they have accounted for approximately 80 percent of the $54 billion foreign direct investment in China since 1978.[11] The home countries of the overseas Chinese have several features in common: all except Thailand have been colonies; all have had governments that do not conform to the Western democratic model; all have a majority or sizable minority of people with a Confucian tradition; and all have a majority or sizable minority of overseas Chinese.[12] Some suggestions for the success of these economies are shown in figure 3.1 and are examined in more detail below.

The Pattern of Overseas Chinese Investment in China

An examination of the pattern of investment suggests that funds from the overseas Chinese have been a major ingredient in the recent economic growth of the southern part of China where, since the "open door" and reform policy was announced 15 years ago, it has become commonplace for them to invest and operate businesses. It is significant that Guangdong, from which the Cantonese—the most numerous of the overseas Chinese groups—originate, has alone received 44.7 percent of all foreign investment in China.[13] Individuals like Gordon Wu, managing director of Hong Kong–based Hopewell Holdings Ltd., have provided concrete assistance in the development of southern China's infrastructure, and many other overseas Chinese tycoons have made large investments. Government advice, as well as commercial and investment assistance, has been made available from Singapore, while Malaysian overseas

Chinese were also quick to increase business ties with their former motherland, once the local government modified its policies. Overseas Chinese in Indonesia have followed suit. The speed and efficiency of this natural process have been remarkable.

Although it is possible to identify some of the major contributions made by the overseas Chinese, for the most part their investments are hidden in such statistics as the 84,000 foreign invested enterprises (FIEs) reported to have been established in China.[14] Overseas Chinese investments are not, for the most part, enterprises large enough to have been publicly identified as equity joint venture (EJV) success stories. Yet the compatriots from Hong Kong have invented a successful, less formal, and more flexible form of EJV—namely, a contract to assemble goods—that was not envisaged in the original EJV law. One study indicates that they operate 25,000 processing factories and employ 3 million workers in Guangdong.[15]

Another area in which overseas Chinese investment particularly stands out is the recently developed Pudong section of Shanghai. According to one expert, "Overseas Chinese have, thus far, been bettered only by the Shanghai government as the main financial support for Pudong." Not only was much of the engineering advice in the early stages of the Pudong project provided by the Chinese-American developer Lin Tongyan, but in April 1992, a subsidiary of the Chia Tai Group of companies—a Thai conglomerate apparently run by ethnic Chinese—signed Pudong's largest investment deal up to that time, valued at $1 billion.[16] Another study found that Hong Kong companies were the largest source of investment in the Shanghai economic zone and accounted for 757 of 1,404 enterprises set up in the area, which had attracted investment of about $5.7 billion. Of this amount, direct foreign capital amounted to $2.9 billion. Taiwanese investors made up the second-largest group.[17]

By using their cultural inner track, the overseas Chinese have been able to put the land and labor of southern China to work more cost-effectively in the short term than other foreign investors, who are usually involved in larger ventures that are more slowly negotiated. Their success is also due to a common written language and culture, an ability to operate in China's underdeveloped legal environment, and "a willingness to play by the rules that would not necessarily be taught at Harvard Business School."[18] Patriotism is cited as an additional spur to investment.[19] Overseas Chinese have, however, tended to be involved in labor-intensive rather than high-technology industries, to the disappointment of the Chinese authorities.[20] The overseas Chinese are also continuing the tradition of contributing to their homeland by transferring remittances, by building schools, and by such spectacular gifts as those from Tan Kah Kee of Singapore, who donated a university to Xiamen (Amoy) before the Japanese War, or from Li Ka-shing of Hong Kong, who endowed a brand-new university complete with a medical school in Shantou in the 1980s.

Hong Kong and the NET: A Special Position

Hong Kong entrepreneurs, as mentioned above, have been especially prominent in the development of their neighboring province of Guangdong, investing above all in property and assembly plants and employing more than 3 million workers there.[21] Today, 80 percent of Hong Kong's manufacturing base lies across the border, and Hong Kong is said to be responsible for 80 percent of the foreign investment in Guangdong.[22] Hong Kong is also involved with infrastructural projects: Gordon Wu's Toll Road is known as a pioneer of the "build-operate-transfer" model, and he and others plan to provide at least six electric generating stations from their Hong Kong base. Most recently, Gordon Wu and his Hopewell Holdings have been negotiating a multimillion-dollar "superhighway" from Guangzhou to Hong Kong.

This type of investment is reflected in the fact that from 1979 to 1991 Guangdong attracted 40 percent of total foreign investment in China and, together with the other four coastal provinces, accounted for two-thirds of the total; Beijing, in contrast, which does not enjoy such strong overseas kinship linkages, attracted only 5 percent of total foreign investment.[23]

Whatever the size of individual investments, the significance of the participation by Chinese from outside China cannot be ignored when the extraordinary growth of Guangdong's economy is taken into consideration. In the last decade, its proportion of China's gross domestic product (GDP) has doubled to 9 percent.[24] These figures are all the more remarkable when it is remembered that the Chinese economy has not remained static, having grown at the impressive average rate of 8.9 percent annually over the last 14 years.[25]

It is certainly not possible to claim that the region's success is due to central government funding. In 1979, Guangdong received 79 percent of its investment funds from Beijing, yet by 1992 Beijing's portion had fallen to 2 percent.[26] Whatever the exact percentage of total investment, therefore, Hong Kong's 75 percent of Guangdong's privately contracted investment indicates that the figure for such investment is undeniably large. Furthermore, it is estimated that Dongguan—a particularly booming area within Guangdong—is the original hometown of about 690,000 of Hong Kong's Chinese residents, or 12 percent of the population. Thus, it may be reasonably assumed that much of this investment comes from Hong Kong.[27]

Overseas Chinese Sources of Investment in the Mainland

Examples of investments by overseas Chinese in mainland enterprises are myriad. The following cases, which have been grouped according to the country from which the funds come, indicate the scope and variety of such activities.

Thailand. The Thai agribusiness conglomerate Charoen Pokphand, owned by Guangdong-born Dhanin Chearavanont, is without a doubt one of the largest foreign investors in China, although "much of the family's business is channelled through private companies operating with the secrecy typical of many Overseas Chinese conglomerates."[28] It is estimated that the group's assets in China total some $1.3 billion, but the executive vice president is keen to point out that, officially, involvement in China is due to monetary, not emotional, considerations: "We invest in China as a business, not out of sentiment."[29]

Singapore. The *South China Morning Post*, when reporting the decision of Robert Kuok of Singapore to buy 34.9 percent of the Hong Kong publishing group that owns the newspaper, carried a diagram of the Kuok business empire's wide-ranging investment in China, including residential and commercial property, Coca-Cola bottling plants, an oil refinery in Guangxi, and a joint venture in vegetable oil plants.[30] Kuok was quoted as giving three reasons for investing in China: to show that there is something good in capitalism; to help to modernize China; and, by promoting prosperity, to help the mainland improve and become more progressive.

More generally, Sino-Singaporean cooperation is strengthening. By the end of 1992, Singapore had invested $1.9 billion in

China, and a cumulative total of 1,371 projects in the mainland had been agreed upon. Moreover, Singapore's investment doubled in 1992, and it was seeking to enter the electric power station field.[31] It appears that investors from Singapore particularly favor Fujian, where they have traditional links.

Indonesia. The position of the overseas Chinese is perhaps more complicated in Indonesia than in any other country in Asia. Close ties with Indonesia's political generals, historically stemming from early support for the anticolonial revolutionary army, have not saved the community from the occasional pogrom, but the strength of some of the main overseas Chinese conglomerates is still great.

One study suggests that the Indonesian Chinese are heavily involved in property, hotels, infrastructure, and airports, particularly in their mother province, Fujian.[32] Indonesia, moreover, houses the largest overseas Chinese conglomerate of all, the Salim Group, which alone represents 5 percent of the country's GDP. Its founder, Liem Sioe Liong, left Fujian in 1937 with nothing and is now in the process of handing over control of a vast empire to his son, Anthony Salim. Another example of the Indonesian overseas Chinese type of international conglomerate is the Lippo Bank, owned by the Riady family, which has developed a major presence in Hong Kong. It owns one of the most conspicuous buildings in the territory, the Lippo Centre. Its activities include banking, finance, insurance, information systems, travel, exhibitions, hotel management, property development, leasing, and manufacturing. Its registered office is in the Cayman Islands, and its advertisements show it operating throughout China, the rest of Asia, the United States, and Australia.

Lippo's 1992 annual report described the group as a substantial contributor to China's development, and tourist, commercial, and property development in Fujian are included in its plans. Its close links with China are illustrated by China Resources's 15 percent share in the group's Hong Kong China Bank and the opening of the bank's joint venture offices in China.[33]

Domestic Attitudes to Investment by Overseas Chinese

China in recent years has encouraged investment from the Overseas Chinese and, indeed, every possible form of economic

contribution from them to the "mother country," and they have
responded vigorously. Some Southeast Asian governments
have, however, taken an unenthusiastic view of this phenomenon.

The Taiwanese government has often made it clear that it
views with concern what it sees as an overlarge volume of
investment by its Chinese population in the mother country—
$19.4 billion between 1984 and 1992.[34] It fears the development of
a situation in which China might have a potent economic
weapon to wield against Taiwan in future political negotiations.
Although Taiwanese investment continues in property and manufacture, investment in mainland real estate and some technology and capital-intensive industries is still banned. More
directly, the largest proposed investment—a petrochemical complex in Fujian—was halted by the Taiwanese government, and
further moves to deter mainland-bound investment have been
signaled by banning the island's largest private steel firm from
collecting funds on the stock market for a multimillion-dollar
mainland project.

In Indonesia, overseas Chinese investment in China has been
noted with disapproval by much of the population. Defenders of
the ethnic Chinese in Indonesia have argued that it is wrong to
classify them as "Chinese" because many of them have declared
themselves Indonesians, but this legalistic interpretation and the
abolition of the Chinese schools have not silenced the complaints
voiced in the local media. The 4.2 million people in Indonesia
who are estimated to be of Han stock are regarded by some other
Indonesians as an alien community with disproportionate
wealth at their disposal.[35] According to the *Economist*, "Indonesia
has a large population of ethnic Chinese and the non-Chinese
majorities tend to be envious of their business".[36] Certainly the
Indonesian president, General Suharto, has come under increasing criticism for allowing the overseas Chinese to dominate the
domestic business scene.

Although Thailand (the only Asian country that was never
colonized) forced its ethnic Chinese community in the 1930s to
adopt Thai names and undergo a Thai education, the level of
Chinese economic power there continues to be a source of fric-
tion.[37] In 1993, a *South China Morning Post* article described the
problems created by the success of the overseas Chinese in Thailand and the resentment of other Thais, observing that although
the overseas Chinese represented only 20 percent of the population, they owned about 50 percent of the wealth of the capital,

Bangkok, and there were complaints that the younger generation of overseas Chinese flaunted their riches.[38]

Generally speaking, the tensions between the overseas Chinese and their adopted countries may be diminishing, in that the younger generation is not as politically attuned as their parents were to the politics of the Chinese mainland and Taiwan.[39] Yet the younger generation of overseas Chinese have continued the philanthropic traditions toward their ancestral origins through investment and commercial and managerial assistance to China, and many families maintain a steady flow of remittances to their relatives. This does, however, contribute to the continuing (even if diminishing) animosity of the indigenous people toward a clearly different Chinese immigrant population with disproportionate wealth that sends large sums out of the territories where it was earned.

Although there is much room for academic debate on the reasons for the success of the overseas Chinese, there is no basic disagreement about their disproportionate wealth in their countries of residence.[40] They are said to control, for instance, more than 40 percent of the private sector in Thailand, and in Indonesia, where they make up 1.6 percent of the population, they are reputed to control 17 of the largest 25 conglomerates and 75 percent of the country's private wealth.[41] Another scholar goes even further, declaring that "almost everywhere in the [Asia] region, the Chinese now appear to be better off than their indigenous neighbors at all income levels."[42]

Conclusions

Given their continuing close ties with their mother country, it is perhaps hardly surprising that once the open door policy was introduced in China, the overseas Chinese invested enthusiastically and continue to do so. It is difficult to imagine that such a development would have occurred in only 15 years without their entrepreneurial drive and the advantages their enterprises derived "from family and ethnic networks which provided them with marketing and management support in their foreign operations."[43]

The overseas contribution to the blossoming of the southern China NET, and indeed to China as a whole, will continue to be of major significance and will expand dynamically for the foreseeable future, with overseas Chinese and mainland resources frequently uniting in successful joint ventures. These successful partnerships are likely to have long-term repercussions, not only throughout East Asia but also much farther afield.

Notes

1. In other literature, I refer to this NET as the South China Economic Community (SCEC). See Sally Stewart, Michael Tow Cheung, and David W. K. Yeung, "The Latest Asian Newly Industrialized Economy (NIE) Emerges: The South China Economic Community," *Columbia Journal of World Business* 27, no. 2 (1992): 30–37.

2. Quoted from a speech given by Milton Friedman at the University of Hong Kong, October 18, 1993.

3. *Time Magazine*, May 10 and 28, 1993; Simon Tam and Gordon Redding, "The Impact of Colonialism on the Formation of an Entrepreneurial Society in Hong Kong," in S. Birley and I.C. MacMillan, eds., S. Subramony, technical ed., *Entrepreneurship Research: Global Perspectives* (The Netherlands: Elsevier Science Publishers, 1993), 158–176.

4. Michael Minor and Hamm B. Curtis, "The 'Little Dragons' as Role Models: Management Implications for China," in Oded Shenkar, ed., *Organization and Management in China 1979–1990* (Armonk, N.Y.: M. E. Sharpe, 1991), 85–95.

5. Guy P. Pfeffermann and Andrea Madarassy, *Trends in Private Investment in Developing Countries 1993: Statistics for 1970–91*, International Finance Corporation Discussion Paper no. 16 (Washington, D.C.: World Bank, 1993).

6. Ibid.

7. Stewart, Cheung, and Yeung, "Latest Asian Newly Industrialized Economy"; G. L. Hicks and S. G. Redding, "The Story of the East Asian 'Economic Miracle,'" *EuroAsia Business Review* no. 3 (1983); Edward K. Y. Chen, *Hyper-Growth in Asian Economies* (London: Macmillan, 1979); Geert Hofstede and Michael Harris Bond, "The Confucius Connection: From Cultural Roots to Economic Growth," *Organizational Dynamics* 16 (Spring 1988): 5–21.; Geert Hofstede, *Cultures and Organizations* (London: McGraw-Hill, 1991); S. G. Redding, *The Spirit of Chinese Capitalism* (New York: Walter de Gruyter, 1990).

8. Hofstede, *Cultures and Organizations*.

9. Victor Limlingan, *The Overseas Chinese in ASEAN: Business Strategies and Management Practices* (Manila: Vita Development Corporation, 1986); Yuan-Li Wu and Chun-Hsi Wu, *Economic Development in Southeast Asia: The Chinese Dimension* (Stanford, Calif.: Hoover Institution, 1980).

10. Hofstede, *Cultures and Organizations*.

11. *Far Eastern Economic Review*, October 21, 1993.

12. Stewart, Cheung, and Yeung, "Latest Asian Newly Industrialized Economy."

13. *China Newsletter* 102 (Tokyo: Japan Economic and Trade Research Organization, February 1993).

14. *Time Magazine*, May 10 and 28, 1993.

15. *South China Morning Post*, May 1, 1993.

16. Lynn T. White, "Joint Ventures in a New Shanghai at Pudong," in Sally Stewart, ed., *Joint Ventures in the People's Republic of China, Advances in Chinese Industrial Studies*, vol. 4 (Greenwich, Conn.: JAI Press, 1994).

17. *South China Morning Post*, November 13, 1993, Business Section, p. 3.

18. *Far Eastern Economic Review*, September 2, 1993.

19. White, "Joint Ventures in a New Shanghai."

20. Ibid.; Sally Stewart, "The Transfer of High Technology to China: Problems and Options" *International Journal of Technology Management*, 3 (1 and 2) (1988): 167–179; and Sally Stewart, "Technology Transfer and the People's Republic of China," in Manas Chatterji, ed., *Technology Transfer in the Developing Countries* (London: MacMillan, 1990), 345–352.

21. *Asia, Inc.* 2, no. 9 (September 1993).

22. *Hong Kong Annual Report 7* (Hong Kong: Hong Kong Government Press, 1993).

23. *Zhongguo Gonyue Jingji Tongji Nianjian* (Beijing: Xinhua Shudian, 1992).

24. Hong Kong Trade Development Council, *Market Profiles on Mainland China's Provinces:13* (Hong Kong: Hong Kong Trade Development Council Research Department, 1992).

25. World Bank, *Trends in Developing Economies* (Washington, D.C.: World Bank, 1992).

26. *Far Eastern Economic Review*, September 2, 1993.

27. David D. Stone, "The Importance of Joint Ventures in the Success of the Guangdong–Hong Kong Economic Miracle," in Stewart, *Joint Ventures in the People's Republic of China*.

28. *Far Eastern Economic Review*, October 21, 1993.

29. Ibid.

30. *South China Morning Post*, September 13, 1993.

31. *China Daily*, May 7, 1993, p. 2.

32. *China Newsletter* 102.

33. *Asia, Inc.* 2, no. 4 (April 1993).

34. *South China Morning Post*, October 6, 1993.

35. Leo Suryadinata, *China and the ASEAN States: The Ethnic Chinese Connection* (Singapore: Singapore University Press, 1985), 6.

36. *Economist*, July 10, 1993.

37. C. P. Fitzgerald, *The Southern Expansion of the Chinese People* (London: Barrie and Jenkins, 1972).

38. *South China Morning Post*, November 13, 1993, Business Section, p. 3.

39. J. Cushman and G. Wang, *Changing Identities of the South East Asian Chinese since World War II* (Hong Kong: University of Hong Kong Press, 1988).

40. Limlingan, *Overseas Chinese in ASEAN*.

41. *Time Magazine*, May 10 and 28, 1993; *Asia, Inc.* 2, no. 8 (August 1993); *Economist*, July 10, 1993.

42. I.A.C. Mackie, "Overseas Chinese Entrepreneurship," *Asian-Pacific Economic Literature* 6 (1992): 1.

43.   H. Zhang and D. Van Den Bulcke, *Chinese Family Owned Multinationals in the Philippines and the Internationalization Process* (Antwerp: Centre for International Management and Development, University of Antwerp, 1993).

4

Princes and Merchant Adventurers: Keeping Bureaucrats Out of Business

J. A. Miller

It is rare that I have the opportunity to discuss trade issues away from the media or the negotiating table, so it is a genuine delight to be able to reflect more informally on the factors that influence trade and investment flows.* My main thesis is not simply that bureaucrats are bad for business, which is an article of Hong Kong's economic creed, but that they are particularly bad for trade in a rapidly globalizing economy.

Since time immemorial international relations have been divided between those devoted to drawing lines on maps and those equally determined to find ways across them—between princes and merchants, or if you prefer, between bureaucrats and businessmen. Nature provides an assortment of natural barriers to trade, some originally deemed impassable, but none has ultimately deterred the merchant in search of profit. Trade, like water, is an irresistible force. It seeks its own level, causing most damage when pent up unnaturally for too long. All the more strange, therefore, that governments seemingly never learn, persisting instead in erecting unnatural barriers to trade and attempting arbitrarily to channel investment in directions it would otherwise never flow.

The growth of trade among Hong Kong, Guangdong, Taiwan, and Fujian provides a near-perfect illustration of this, because the surge in the flow of capital and goods has happened largely in spite of government intervention rather than because of it. Before turning to Hong Kong's perspective on the economic dynamics in this area, I will discuss some specific facets of the

* This chapter is based on a luncheon address given by the author to participants at the Pacific Forum CSIS conference entitled "Economic Interdependence and the Nation-State: The Emergence of the Natural Economic Territory in Southern China, Taiwan, and Hong Kong," held April 17–19, 1994, in Hong Kong.

global economic system that provide a relevant backdrop to economic policies in the southern China natural economic territory (NET).

Global Business versus Local Government

One of the great ironies of the information age is that although it has encouraged businesses to think globally, it often compels governments to act parochially. Despite the collective wisdom of experience, the first resort of politicians when faced with essentially domestic economic problems is to raise the bogey of the external threat. As a result, to paraphrase an eminent economist of the early part of this century, they often end up doing to their partners in peace what they do to their enemies in war: they impose trade sanctions.

And, not unnaturally, while some entrepreneurs are happy to mix in the global marketplace, others feel threatened. So also do farmers, entrenched unions, and other inwardly focused advocates of "un-change." Armed with information on the "low wages," "unspeakable working conditions," and other supposed advantages available to foreign competitors, they have shown a remarkable ability to bend governments to their will. Against the better judgment of intelligent politicians, against the interests of consumers, and at considerable cost to the domestic economy in terms of consequent structural maladjustment, their views all too often prevail over their fellow nationals who unpatriotically invest abroad.

In addition to trade sanctions, antidumping legislation has become more widely used and is increasingly complex. Yet surely it is decreasingly relevant in a world where businesses source components internationally, assemble them frequently in more than one place, and market them globally. In such a world, does it matter where things are made? With the progressive reduction in tariff barriers, it would make more sense to raise revenue from sales and profits taxes and leave customs services free to concentrate on the illegal trade in such social threats as drugs and armaments.

Discussions in multilateral forums are beginning to turn the spotlight on some of these paradoxes in the traditional trade paradigm, in particular the definition of "national interest." The prevalence of mercantilist thought in even the most advanced of developed countries is nowhere more striking than in the contrast between competition and trade policy. In the former, consumers and their interests reign supreme. In the latter, they find themselves disenfranchised by producers. The resulting transfer of wealth from the pockets of consumers and taxpayers to the bank balances of farmers and businessmen is an astonishing perversion of the democratic process.

Trade Blocs and Mental Blocks

The postwar international trading system, embodied in the General Agreement on Tariffs and Trade (GATT) and now the World Trade Organization (WTO), is founded on brilliantly simple principles—most-favored-nation (MFN) status, national treatment, and transparency—that have worked well when allowed to. Some governments, however, frustrated with the slow speed of change in GATT and impelled by other strategic imperatives, have tried to improve on it by experimenting with more-localized attempts at managing trade liberalization. Such arrangements are a poor second-best to the GATT multilateral system because they substitute reciprocity for the equity that flows from MFN treatment.

These attempts to manage trade have a number of weaknesses, of which the following are the more significant:

- They define the limits of freedom rather than the potential for increasing it.
- External trade policies tend to be dictated by the lowest internal common denominator.
- Businesses are distracted from external markets by the need to carve out and then defend internal market share.
- They encourage acceptance of the fallacy that geographically contiguous areas are more natural trading partners than those that are not.
- They encourage imitation.

The European Community (now the European Union) provides a convenient morality play for illustrating these dangers of trade and investment distortion. During the period 1961 to 1991, member states increasingly traded with one another at the expense of their share of the external world market. Member states' exports to one another increased from 43 percent to 62 percent of world exports while the share of EC exports to third markets fell from 20 percent to 15 percent. To borrow a phrase from Martin Wolf, member states were "too often taking in one another's high-cost washing, while failing to sustain their global competitiveness." In the run-up to the Single Market, European businesses concentrated on positioning themselves to secure a larger share of the restricted market, to which they would have privileged access, rather than competing on equal terms for a share of the global market. If businessmen are thus inclined to preempt the plans of governments, it is doubly important that bureaucrats should be careful not to distort their perceptions of reality.

The Southern China NET: Keeping Bureaucrats out of Business

Looking at the extraordinary developments in this part of the world from a purely Hong Kong perspective, the adjustment required since Deng Xiaoping's farsighted and courageous decision to reopen the People's Republic of China to trade and investment has been savage. The challenge, though of a different scale, has been similar to the challenge to Europe following the end of the cold war, and the adjustment has been just as painful. Hong Kong's industry faced a sudden change in comparative advantage across the border. In the space of only 10 short years Hong Kong's manufacturing workforce halved, and inflation was pushed to uncomfortably high levels for several years. This was fueled in part by fierce competition for the scarce white-collar skills needed to service the demands of trading with a new and rapidly developing hinterland.

Many have asked whether these events are threatening: surely Hong Kong's industry is being hollowed out, surely it will become unduly dependent on China. I confess that I find nothing threatening in any of this; quite the reverse.

We in Hong Kong are witnessing the adjustment of three separate economies, or four counting Macao, marked by the gradual removal of the totally unnatural barriers erected in the early 1950s. In Hong Kong's case it was the embargo on trade with China, imposed by the United Nations during the Korean War, that abruptly shut off our natural entrepôt role. Forty years later, we are in the process of regaining that role and doing so from a position of economic strength, for we have developed sophisticated manufacturing and financial sectors in the unnaturally insulated interim.

Hong Kong has not stopped manufacturing. Output has increased by 80 percent over the same period as it has moved up the technology and value-added scale. Yet would it matter if it had fallen? Hong Kong has not suffered from unemployment—rather, overall employment has been uncomfortably tight, as workers have slipped into new service sector jobs. Hong Kong has moved from being a mainly manufacturing economy to primarily a service economy. Services now account for close to 80 percent of Hong Kong's gross domestic product, with financial and business services alone accounting for 25 percent. Our success in achieving the transition back to our natural role as smoothly as we have owes much to the deliberate policy of the Hong Kong government to do nothing either to impede or to direct the process of adjustment.

The success and swiftness of the wider regional adjustment can be attributed to a similar circumstance: on the whole it has been business-led and not government-directed. Necessity has played a part—communications between China and Taiwan have long been difficult at an official level. Bureaucratic choice has also played a part—development outside the Special Economic Zones owes much to encouragement from southern Chinese officials to the townsfolk of the delta and elsewhere to go it alone. So, too, have farsighted business initiatives by those businessmen—such as Gordon Wu, Li Ka-shing, and Peter Woo—who are increasingly familiar with China's needs and are skilled in assembling capital for heavy infrastructure development. (Imagine the delays if we had to rely on a joint planning commission!) Far more important than any of these, however, have been the countless decisions of individual entrepreneurs and traders finding their way across newly porous borders.

In short, I do not see anything threatening in any of this, any more than I regard the wider globalization of the world economy as in any way a threat to the nation-state. What is happening in southern China, where history has left a complex constitutional legacy, is economically no different from what is happening in northern China. There both Korean and Japanese firms are busy working out an essentially similar market-driven industrial restructuring.

Ultimately, how one views globalization depends on a perception of the proper limits of government's role. If globalization is a threat to anything, I sincerely hope that it imperils the old trade paradigm I mentioned earlier—the paradigm that insists on giving a national identity to products for the purpose of protection and, in the process, allows the substitution of bureaucratic regulation for commercial competition. That paradigm has outlived its usefulness and now serves only to impede modern patterns of production and capital flows, creating waste rather than increasing the world's plenty. The closing years of the twentieth century have seen the triumph of the market over centrally planned economies at the national level. The challenge as we enter the new millennium is to ensure that the market triumphs internationally as well, in the victory of free trade over managed trade or, in the terms in which I opened, a victory of business over bureaucracy.

5

Ask a Tiger for Its Hide? Taiwan's Approaches to Economic Transactions across the Strait

Milton D. Yeh

Since the end of the 1980s, the expansion of economic activities between Taiwan and the People's Republic of China has resulted primarily from China's reform policies and secondarily from Taiwan's mainland policy. China's "economic districts," or Special Economic Zones (SEZs), attracted Taiwanese businesses at a time of unexpectedly rising manufacturing costs in Taiwan. Lower land and wage costs, the enormous internal market, and fewer environmental concerns in China were all factors in the trend of growing economic ties.

Recognizing these comparative advantages on the opposite sea shore—the Chinese mainland—the Taiwanese make two kinds of evaluation. Focusing on business considerations, some Taiwanese are positively inclined toward the possible benefits China's "open door" policy offers. Others perceive the Chinese Communists as an awakening "lion" whose behavior is unpredictable and thus give warning with the Chinese saying, "Ask a tiger for its hide?" This warning implies that a deal with the Chinese Communists has uncertain results and will be a risky business and, in most cases, an impossible mission.

The profitability and form of economic transactions across the Taiwan Strait, and subsequent benefit to the Taiwanese as a whole, have been hotly debated in Taiwan in recent years. This chapter first presents the two arguments outlined above. Then I analyze some of the policy instruments the Taiwan government has adopted in response to this trend. In addition, I shall briefly analyze the political and economic factors that condition the relationships among Taiwan, mainland China, and Hong Kong.

Trade Interaction

Because it is technically difficult for the Taipei authorities to ban exports to the mainland, Taiwan's government has been focusing principally on regulating imports from the mainland

and only secondarily on the export market. Taiwanese exports to the mainland first started to climb as a result of Beijing's unilateral decision in 1978 to allow Taiwanese trade via Hong Kong or Macao. Taiwan's official response seemed to be a calculated one: not until July 1985 did it lift the trade embargo against China and permit indirect trade. Yet it strictly regulated imports and still prevented Taiwanese from establishing any contact with Chinese organizations or people.[1]

In May 1990, Taiwan dramatically changed its policies regarding imports from the mainland and allowed importation via Hong Kong of 155 categories of raw materials, primarily medical herbs, fish, fine feathers, antibiotics, minerals, cotton, and lumber.[2] Significantly, the government deliberately chose items that could be obtained elsewhere to minimize the damage that would be caused by a sudden cutoff of supplies from China. By 1993, the Ministry of Economic Affairs (MEA) was allowing a total of 1,654 products to be imported from the mainland, one-fifth of which were semifinished.[3] In 1995, the Foreign Trade Bureau of the MEA was scheduled to waive import licenses.

It is difficult to determine if Taiwan's mainland imports will increase as restrictions are removed because trade will still be required to go through Hong Kong. In other words, Taipei's indirect trade policy is still conditioned by political considerations. Given China's unceasing attempts to downgrade the Taiwan government to the status of a local authority, Taipei's concerns about territorial security and full jurisdiction over its territory remain central in its trade and investment policies. For Taiwan, direct trade with the mainland will necessitate direct navigation across the strait, thereby obscuring the territorial demarcation between Taiwan and the mainland. As long as the Taipei authorities perceive direct trade as a potential threat to Taiwan's territorial security, they will maintain the indirect trade policy.[4]

Yet indirect trade entails higher costs than direct trade, and businessmen are putting growing pressure on the government to liberalize trade policy, partly by headquartering their businesses outside Taiwan. For Taiwanese businessmen running small-scale sunset industries, such as footwear or umbrellas, who move their entire assembling plants to mainland China, the existence of direct or indirect transportation links across the Taiwan Strait seems less significant. Businesses in the service sector, such as banking, shipping, and airlines, and large business syndicates whose operations are highly dependent on legal frameworks and resource allocation from governmental agencies take a wait-and-see attitude toward the government's mainland policy but focus most of their efforts on research only. It is among the businesses that manufacture semifinished products in mainland China and import them back to Taiwan to process into finished products that concern is greatest for a direct navigation route across the strait. This direct-indirect navigation debate erupted in early 1994, when Taiwan's minister of economic affairs, Chiang Pin-kung, proposed permitting port-to-port direct shipping links across the strait "to establish an industrial division-of-labor network and thereby to rationalize economic and trade relations across the strait." In elaborating his reasoning, Minister Chiang stressed that this network would "allow the ROC to reap the benefits of a complementary division of labor and help Taiwan enterprises rooted on the island of Taiwan."

Chiang also pointed out, however, that this framework for cooperation between Taiwan and the mainland was still blocked by China's "unfriendly response" to Taiwan's activities in the international community. Because port-to-port direct shipping will inevitably lead to overall shipping and aviation links across the Taiwan Strait and make it difficult for the MEA alone to effectively regulate economic transactions, academic circles opposed Chiang's proposal. Responding to Chiang's suggestion, the Mainland Affairs Council (MAC) commented that Chiang's proposal should be weighed not merely in economic terms but also in terms of border security and related social costs. Soon thereafter, Chiang withdrew his proposal, stating in a report to the Legislative Yuan's Committee on Economic Affairs that he would pool opinions from the MAC as well as from the Ministry of Transportation.[5]

Investment Flows

The Taiwan government allows indirect investment through four mechanisms: establishment of company branches in a third district, investment in companies in a third district, investment through companies in territories outside the mainland, and investment in mainland China through indirect remittances. Companies are allowed to invest in China's foreign exchange, machinery equipment and component parts, raw materials, semifinished products and finished products, professional techniques (patents, trademarks, and copyrights), profits from foreign investments, and technical cooperation.[6] Investment projects of $3 million must register with the MEA's Screening Investment Committee; failure to do so entails a fine of $120,000 to $600,000.[7]

The Taiwan government prohibits investment in four categories: defense technologies, products that are fully or are partially researched and designed by the government, and products that are prohibited for sale to mainland China by international organizations. Nevertheless, by June 1993, 3,155 cases of other types of investment totaling $3 billion had been directed to the mainland. The investment in order of magnitude was in electronics, the food industry, plastics, rubber, metals, precision machinery, clothing, construction, and textiles. The majority of investment was directed to Guangzhou, Shanghai, and Shenzhen with additional projects in Xiamen and Fujian.[8]

Strictly speaking, however, it has been difficult for the Taiwan government to block the outflow of capital to the mainland. In fact, Taiwanese businessmen can take capital out of the territory either by purchasing so-called traveling exchange or transferring foreign exchange earned from exports, because each Taiwanese is allowed to exchange up to $3 million annually. There are so many ways for exporters to retain foreign exchange in the mainland that it has been estimated that the total foreign exchange from exports not changed to new Taiwan dollars expanded from $2.89 billion in 1987 to $24 billion in 1991.[9]

Official views on the effect on the island economy of Taiwanese investment in the mainland obviously differ from those of private entrepreneurs. The Taiwan government worries that the effect may be to hollow out Taiwan's industry. According to research, however, this has never occurred. A survey sponsored by the Industrial Development Bureau and based on interviews with 140 Taiwanese companies indicated that cross-strait investment has "to some extent" pushed local manufacturers to invest more in research and development (R&D). It found that the business turnover of those firms has risen by an average of 33.5 percent in the past few years. Those companies interviewed have also largely increased their R&D funds and personnel at their home bases on Taiwan. According to the survey, 92.1 percent of the respondents said they usually accept orders in Taiwan and produce the goods at their mainland plants for export. Although 55.7 percent said their mainland plants produce only components, parts, or semifinished goods for assembly in Taiwan, some 33 percent reported that their mainland plants manufacture the same products as their Taiwan factories. The study also

Table 5.1
Industrial Manufacturing in Taiwan, 1987–1991

	1987	1991
Percentage of total manufacturing:		
Light industry	35.14	28.16
Heavy industry	38.01	41.61
Chemical industry	26.82	30.32
Productivity index:		
Precision machinery	114.80	151.92

Source: Chien Ching-chang, "An Analysis of Taiwanese Investment to the Mainland," *Newsletter on Economy, Trade Across the Straits (NETAS)*, January 10, 1993, no. 13, pp. 3–6.

found that the financing of 68.5 percent of Taiwan-invested mainland plants is handled by their parent company on Taiwan.[10]

A second study supports the conclusion that not only did the hollowing-out effect on industry not occur, but that there has been a shift away from labor-intensive to capital-intensive industries.[11] As seen in table 5.1, from 1987 on, nearly all labor-intensive light industries have been substantially reduced (not including those industries deemed "essential," such as food, drink, and tobacco), while capital-intensive and high-technology industries have expanded.

Political Constraints on Cross-Taiwan Strait Economic Flows

As previously mentioned, businessmen and academic researchers in Taiwan have not been concerned about the possible negative effects of Taiwanese investment on the mainland. In contrast, officials have been concerned about Beijing's expansionist political attitudes toward Taiwan. Beijing's "one China" notion, combining military threat and diplomatic defense, represses Taiwan's motivation to cooperate with China in the economic sphere.

China's constant efforts to cut off Taiwan's sources of arms—
despite its own aggressive arms buildup—have been reflected
in several events. At the Seattle summit of the Asia-Pacific Economic Cooperation forum in November 1993, Chinese Communist leader Jiang Zemin complained to President Bill Clinton
about his predecessor's decision to sell 150 F-16 fighters to Taiwan and demanded a promise that the United States would not
allow new sales. In the same month, Beijing made the same
request to German chancellor Helmut Kohl when he visited the
mainland. And in January 1994, China and France simulta-
neously announced a communiqué in which Paris agreed not to
authorize any new arms sales to Taiwan.

China has also had success in isolating Taiwan diplomatically, for instance when it announced in January 1994 the establishment of diplomatic relations with Lesotho, which had
maintained formal links with Taipei since 1990. This leaves the
total number of countries that have formal ties with Taiwan at
only 28.[12]

Facing China's constant effort to suppress and squeeze Taiwan out of the international community, the opposition Democratic People's Party (DPP) urged the Mainland Affairs Council
to make its "mainland policy" clear enough to convince Taiwanese businessmen not to invest in the mainland, arguing that this
activity strengthened China's ability to implement dollar diplomacy against Taiwan in the international community. Minister
of Foreign Affairs Frederick Chien warned that Beijing's
attempts to isolate Taiwan diplomatically and its efforts to prevent the sale of defensive weapons to Taiwan clearly demonstrated that the Chinese Communists' threat to Taiwan's security
had not changed, despite the thaw in relations. Minister Chien
maintained that to protect Taiwan's interests, future relations
with Beijing must not be hurriedly improved on the Taiwan side
alone but should proceed cautiously.[13]

Although the Straits Exchange Foundation (SEF) in Taipei
and the Association for Relations Across the Taiwan Straits
(ARATS) sponsored the Koo-Wang talks—representing the first
interaction between the two regimes after four decades of military confrontation—the three meetings held during April 1993
and March 1994 failed to produce any concrete agreements.[14]
The main agenda items were the repatriation of illegal immigrants and hijackers and cross-strait fishing disputes. The two
sides remain locked in political disputes over such fundamental
issues as the perception of sovereignty. Thus, neither the SEF nor

ARATS, acting as semiofficial liaison agents, has been able to arrive at any agreement helpful in promoting economic transactions across the strait.

In response to Beijing's efforts to isolate Taiwan, Taipei has initiated a "southward policy" to secure its political and economic ties with southeast Asian nations. In a weeklong vacation to Malaysia and Singapore during the 1994 New Year holiday, Premier Lien Chan held private talks with his counterparts as well as with other high-ranking government officials. During the ensuing lunar festival holiday, President Lee Teng-hui brought a sizable delegation of officials to Bali, Indonesia, and Phukit, Thailand, via the Subic Bay airport in the Philippines and held private conversations with his counterparts. In additional efforts, several delegations of Taiwanese economic officials have visited Vietnam and Indonesia to explore cooperation.

Some have interpreted this southward policy as an attempt by the Taiwan government to cool down "mainland fever." Yet, this policy must be viewed in the context of Taipei's larger goal of developing Taiwan as a center for regional economic activities and, thus, as complementary to and not a restraint on its mainland policy.

In fact, the Taiwanese authorities realize that it is impossible to hold back the island's increasing trade dependence on mainland China, and the MEA still emphasizes the mainland's potential. The chairman of the cabinet's Council for Economic Planning and Development (CEPD), Vincent Siew, has even proposed to actively engage mainland China in positioning Taiwan as a trade and shipping hub for mainland China as well as for Indochina. Siew's proposal would establish a "golden triangle" of economic territories among Taipei, Shanghai, and Singapore to promote economic cooperation in such areas as transportation and technology. In essence, Siew's proposal advocates two goals: to establish vertical cooperation between parent companies in Taiwan and their assembly lines on the mainland in order to maintain the comparative advantage of Taiwan's export industry; and to promote the internationalization of Taiwanese companies by establishing Taipei as a shipping and trading hub for mainland China and Indochina as well.

Compared with Chiang Pin-kung's option for port-to-port links across the Taiwan Strait mentioned earlier, Siew's grand approach seems to be well received politically. Should Chiang's port-to-port direct links be realized, some sort of symbolic economic "unification" between Taiwan and the mainland would bring political difficulties for the Kuomintang in meeting the challenge from the DPP, which for the moment still declines to be involved, however slightly, in the affairs of the Chinese regime. Relatively speaking, then, Siew's concept of a golden-triangle economic territory among Taipei, Shanghai, and Singapore seems, at least symbolically, to modify the character of "unification" between Taiwan and the mainland and is thereby a less political approach than Chiang's.[15]

How soon and to what extent Siew's proposal is implemented is still to be seen. At present, a large volume of economic transactions across the Taiwan Strait is processed through Hong Kong, and its role in facilitating cross-straits economic flows should not be underestimated.

Taiwan and Hong Kong

Given Taiwan's "indirect economic exchange" model, which relies on Hong Kong as a third district, exchanges between Hong Kong and Taiwan have become significant since the early 1980s. Total trade in 1993 reached $20.18 billion, or 12.4 percent of Taiwan's total trade. Hong Kong is the largest market for Taiwan's exports, and Taiwan's exports to Hong Kong reached $18.45 billion, or 21.7 percent of Taiwan's total exports.

In the past four decades, the relationship between Taipei and Hong Kong has been conditioned by the United Kingdom's "China policy," which has made it difficult for Taipei to maintain an official relationship with Hong Kong. Taipei authorities have for a long time treated Hong Kong citizens as overseas Chinese and implemented their overseas Chinese policy to absorb capital from Hong Kong. When they operate businesses in Taiwan, Hong Kong businessmen, like other overseas Chinese, receive certain tax exemptions and preferential treatment in purchasing production equipment, procuring loans, and transferring remittances and personal assets. As a result, from 1952 through 1991, investment by Hong Kong Chinese in Taiwan totaled $630.4 billion, or about one-third of the total overseas Chinese investment in Taiwan.

In the late 1980s, the Taiwan government chose Hong Kong as a "third district" in implementing its new mainland policy. Whereas the pace and scope of economic cooperation between Taiwan and Hong Kong had been conditioned by the British China policy in the past, it was to be constrained again by Beijing's involvement in the internal affairs of Hong Kong.

Recent events show that Beijing's authorities deliberately choose a strategically important issue to get involved in and thereby dictate the policy formulation of the Hong Kong government. For example, to attract Taiwanese investment or simply to pursue its "united front" goal, Beijing has repeatedly claimed that all of Taipei's semiofficial agents stationed in Hong Kong be kept in operation even after July 1, 1997. Meanwhile, the Chinese regime has also urged its agents in Hong Kong to promote joint ventures between mainlanders and Taiwanese via Hong Kong. In contrast, however, when Taipei proposed to negotiate directly with the Hong Kong government to renew the aviation contract that was due to expire in June 1995, Beijing objected and requested that any party that wanted to negotiate with Taipei on aviation matters consult Beijing's authorities.[16] Thus, the more Beijing is involved in the operation of Hong Kong, the greater will be the uncertainties in Taiwan-Hong Kong relations.

Conclusion

In the aftermath of the cold war, it is obvious that the regimes on either side of the Taiwan Strait find no rationale for engaging in costly military confrontation with each other and focus instead on the mutual benefit of the burgeoning export industry. To date, however, China's expansionist policy has mainly driven the process, so that Taiwan must use high-cost indirect routes for processing its trade and investment to the mainland.

In any event, the Ministry of Economic Affairs has indeed constantly and cautiously permitted Taiwanese businessmen to move their assembly plants to mainland China and maintain their headquarters in Taiwan. This vertical division of labor across the Taiwan Strait is in Taiwan's favor. In the long term, however, as China becomes more competitive in the world market, the question is how Taiwan can maintain its competitiveness. In this regard, then, whether for economic or diplomatic considerations, the idea of establishing Taipei as a processing center in Asia is probably a valuable goal deserving Taiwan's attention.

The degree to which international factors matter is still unclear. In the years to come, if both regimes are granted membership in the World Trade Organization (WTO) and the Beijing authorities indeed abide by the norms and regulations of the WTO, the potential market would certainly become an impetus for speeding up economic integration among the "three Chinas."

Notes

1. Chang Jorng-feng, "An Analysis of the Facts of the Entrepôt Trade via Hong Kong across the Straits," *Chung-Kuo ta-lu yan-chiu* (Mainland China Studies) (Taipei) 31, no. 8 (February 1989): 42–43.

2. Ministry of Economic Affairs, Taipei, *Ta-lu T'ou-tzu yu ching-mao tzu-hsun* (Information Monthly on Mainland Investment, Economy and Trade, or IMMIET), no. 7, 1991, pp. 2–9.

3. Straits Exchange Foundation, Taipei, *Liang-an Ching-mao T'ung-hsun* (Newsletter on Economy, Trade Across the Strait, or NETAS), no. 10, 1993, pp. 6–8.

4. Milton D. Yeh, "Politics of Trilateral Trade among Mainland China, Hong Kong and Taiwan," in Kuang-sheng Liao, ed., *The New International Order in East Asia* (Hong Kong: The Chinese University of Hong Kong, 1993), 177.

5. For newspaper accounts of Chiang's statements, see *China Times,* January 3, 1994, p. 19; *China Post,* January 22, 1994, p. 1; *China Times,* January 15, 1994, p. 4; *China News,* January 21, 1994, p. 1; *Chinese Daily,* March 24, 1994, p. 4.

6. *NETAS,* no. 9, September 10, 1992, p. 5.

7. *NETAS,* no. 19, July 10, 1993, p. 7.

8. Ibid., pp. 6–7.

9. Chien Ching-chang, "An Analysis of Taiwanese Investment to the Mainland," *NETAS,* no. 13, January 10, 1993, p. 4.

10. *China News,* January 24, 1994, p. 16.

11. Chien, "Analysis," p. 4.

12. *China Post,* January 14, 1994, p. 4.

13. For newspaper accounts of the DPP and Minister Chien's proposals, see *China Times,* January 15, 1994, p. 2; *China News,* January 21, 1994, p. 3; *Free Times,* January 15, 1994, p. 1.

14. For additional details on the Koo-Wang talks, see note 20 in chapter 1.

15. For newspaper accounts of Siew's proposal, see *China Post,* January 7, 1994, p. 1; *China Times,* February 19, 1991, p. 6; *China Times,* January 6, 1994, p. 2; *China Times,* February 20, 1994, p. 2.

16. *China Times,* July 29, 1994, p. 9; August 16, 1994, p. 1.

6

Effect of the Natural Economic Territory on China's Economic and Political Strategies

Chen Dezhao

This chapter begins with an overview of the People's Republic of China's "open" areas and their dynamics over the past 15 years, followed by analyses of the overall economic expansion in southern China and the policies designed to address the resultant problems of further economic growth in the region. The chapter concludes with a discussion of possible lessons for the development of natural economic territories (NETs) for other regions in China and elsewhere in the world.

Overview

A multi-tiered, multi-channeled, omnidirectional structural opening has taken shape in China during the past 15 years (1979–1994). Originating along the coastal areas, the opening then expanded along China's major rivers, followed by the country's borders, and has gradually encompassed nearly all of the capitals of the inland provinces or autonomous regions of ethnic minorities.

The coastal open areas constitute a three-part, closely inter-locked system, which includes the following regions.

- The "frontlands," composed of the five Special Economic Zones (SEZs) of Shenzhen, Zhuhai, Shantou, Xiamen, and Hainan Island.

- The "hubs," made up of 14 open coastal port cities, including Fuzhou, Guangzhou, Shanghai, Tianjin, Qingdao, and Ningbo.

- The "rear," made up of the coastal open economic areas, which were designated in February 1985 and include the Changjiang (Yangtze River) delta, the Pearl River delta, and the delta area of Xiamen, Zhangzhou, and Quianzhou in southern Fujian Province. Thus far, the rear has greatly expanded to include the coastal parts of the provinces of Hebei (2 cities and 12 counties), Liaoning (7 cities and 16 counties), Jiangsu (7 cities and 40 counties), Zhejiang (5 cities and 29 counties), Fujian (4 cities and 33 counties), Shandong (6 cities and 25 counties), and Guangdong (15 cities and 42 counties); Guangxi Zhuangzu Autonomous Region (one city and 5 counties); and counties under the jurisdiction of Shanghai (6) and Tianjin (5).

Since Deng Xiaoping's famous inspection tour of southern China in the spring of 1992, China has opened its doors even more widely to the outside world. In March of the same year, 13 cities and towns along the country's borders in the provinces or autonomous regions of Heilongjiang, Jilin, and Inner Mongolia in the North and Yunnan and Guangxi in the South were, for the first time, declared open to overseas trade and investment. Four months later, the pace of opening quickened, and additional areas were declared open. These include five cities along the Changjiang, such as Chongqing in Sichuan Province; seven capitals of provinces or autonomous regions along the seaboard, such as Harbin and Changchun in the northeast; and 11 capitals of inland provinces and autonomous regions, such as Chengdu in Sichuan, Xian in Shanxi, and Yinchuan in Ningxia.

Southern China in the Overall Economy

Three unique features can be discerned from the above sketch. First, compared with the early 1980s when the five SEZs were launched, the areas now open to the outside world have expanded to more than half a million square kilometers, involving 339 cities and counties and a population of more than 300 million. The growth of the southern China economic area and the resultant problems, all local in nature, can be examined and understood only in the context of this overall picture.

Second, China's opening continues to be a gradual process. Great discrepancies exist in natural conditions and levels of social and economic development among different parts of the country. Considering that there are certain requirements for becoming an open area in terms of economic and technological levels, resources, transportation, telecommunications, and living facilities, China decided to select those better qualified in such fields to be pioneers. Inevitably, frictions arose between pioneers and followers due to differences in the timing, degree, speed, and scope of opening. However, similarities still exist in terms of promoting the country's openness among all the open areas, whether they be in coastal China (Guangdong and Fujian) or in the hinterland.

Third, opening up to the outside world has obviously stimulated the economic development of China as a whole. Benefiting from closer economic links with Hong Kong, Macao, and Taiwan, southern China has been running faster—but this does not mean that other parts of the country have stayed still. The 15 years of reform and opening have seen the fastest economic development in the country's long history, and the problems induced by the economic progress of southern China result from troubles between high fliers and relatively slow runners. All are moving ahead, with no sluggards. These three features are all related to government remedies and their effects.

The Widening Gap

Southern China has acted as a locomotive in spurring on other parts of the country in the economic race. Thus, common interests dominate in intraprovincial and local-center relations. There is, however, the other side of the coin. Wranglings have flared up between southern China and other parts of the country as well as between southern China and the center. Two aspects of these relationships merit attention.

One aspect concerns preferential treatment in taxation for the open areas (such as income tax and customs rates). For example, overseas investors in the SEZs have enjoyed preferential treatment in generally paying only a 15 percent income tax, whereas the corresponding rate for state enterprises was 55 percent and 24 percent for non-SEZ open areas or cities prior to 1994. In addition, export enterprises in the SEZs using imported raw materials are exempt from paying customs duties, product taxes, and value-added taxes. Overseas investors who come to the SEZs for investment or business negotiations can also enjoy preferential treatment in simplified procedures for entry or exit. Furthermore, SEZ administrations have been granted greater decision-making power in foreign business operations and more latitude in approving foreign-funded projects. Thus, regions and enterprises elsewhere are not competing with the SEZs on level ground. What is more, preferential tax treatment for the SEZs meant tax losses for the central government.

It is no wonder that clashes of interests over such matters became aggravated. A comparison between Shanghai and the SEZs in Guangdong may drive the point home. In the late 1980s, on average, Shanghai turned over to the state budget more than 10 billion yuan annually in the form of tax revenues and state enterprise profits; yet the corresponding figure for Guangdong Province was just somewhat over 1 billion, or one-tenth of that for Shanghai. Guangdong even lagged behind Guangzhou, its own provincial capital, in terms of tax revenue contributions to the center. In 1991, the central government ran a financial deficit of 18.2 billion yuan. This deficit could have been largely offset or even eliminated just by denying the SEZs preferential tax treatment.

The second important aspect in intraprovincial relations concerns the ever-widening gap between southern China and inland provinces in the level of economic development. In 1993, the seven coastal provinces accounted for 70 percent of the volume of additional national growth. In the first quarter of 1994, the growth rates for eastern, central, and western China were 21 percent, 15 percent, and less than 10 percent, respectively. Thus, imbalances in regional development have been worsening with each passing day. Further, capital outflows from less-developed to developed regions were on the rise in 1993 in pursuit of quicker and higher returns. Moreover, closer economic links with Hong Kong led to relatively larger exports for Guangdong and Fujian. These two provinces therefore paid higher prices for buying raw materials in the interior, and Fujian even resorted to setting up checkpoints to stem the outflow of local raw materials, thereby hindering the evolution of a unified national market.

These imbalances in regional economic development have resulted in strong demands from the inland provinces for leveling the playing field. Some have been calling for less-preferential treatment for the open areas, but the majority have been clamoring for an equal share. The central government finally sided with the majority by adopting two sets of policy measures. First, the center declared more and more areas open to foreign trade and investment by granting them preferential treatment in taxation. For example, open cities and areas in the interior now also enjoy a 24 percent preferential tax rate in terms of enterprise income tax. The so-called sci-tech street in the Haidian district of suburban Beijing even enjoys a 15 percent preferential tax rate on a par with the SEZs. Meanwhile, a second policy initiative on January 1, 1994, unified the income tax rate at 33 percent for all enterprises funded by domestic investment, regardless of location, effectively reducing the income tax by 22 percent for all inland state enterprises. These two sets of policy measures are designed to benefit the economic expansion of inland areas and enterprises, thereby laying the foundation for enhanced state tax revenues. But in the short term, they reduce state revenues and strain even more an already tight financial situation in the center.

The widening gap between coastal China and the interior could worsen in the foreseeable future as provinces like Guangdong and Fujian keep surging ahead. Despite considerable financial subsidies and other forms of support to the hinterland, the central government is in no position to narrow the widening gap. This is indeed a crucial concern in China's future economic development.

Why the Separation of Southern China Is Impossible

The worrisome trend noted above has its limits. The line will be drawn at southern China's secession or transformation into an independent economic area or group because of closer economic ties with Hong Kong, Macao, and Taiwan or its own explosion of growth. The reasoning can be traced to the following factors.

- In political and social terms, despite their preferential economic treatment and privileges, the coastal areas remain under the control of a unified national party and military leadership. Whether they are in Guangdong, Fujian, or other open areas, the local committees of the Chinese Communist Party and other democratic parties are obliged to obey the orders of their respective central committees. Similarly, local military units are under the control of the Central Military Commission of the Central Committee of the Communist Party of China. Indeed, many cases of local partition short of formal separation have occurred in China's history; yet these cases have always been with the actions of local warlords. A local partition would be unthinkable in the absence of local warlordism.

- In the area of policy-making, the ultimate authority rests with the central government, the plethora of policy privileges for open areas like Guangdong and Fujian notwithstanding. Unlike the states of the United States, Chinese provinces are not members of a federation and, generally speaking, are not vested with legislative power. The case of the Hainan SEZ is somewhat different because it has been vested with larger legislative powers. With the exception of functions under unified central control such as foreign affairs, public security, border defense, customs houses, and civil aviation, the Hainan SEZ may formulate local rules and regulations in light of specific local conditions. Yet this legislative power does not derive from relevant constitutional articles. Rather, it has to be granted by the National People's Congress, the highest legislative authority of the country.

- The ultimate authority for approval of large projects—those with capital investment of more than 100 million yuan—also rests with the center. The governments of open areas, whether in Guangdong or Fujian, have no decision-making power over the launching or dismantling of these enterprises or projects.

- Major infrastructure development projects, such as construction of rail lines, arterial highways, major ports, airfields, and postal communications, depend on state investment, and their management is also mainly in the hands of the center.

- Last but not least, apart from the political, economic, and social factors listed above, coastal open areas like Fujian and Guangdong constitute an integral component of a unified national market. They simply cannot hope to stay outside this evolving giant single market. Along with deepening reform and bolder opening, the central government is devising a number of instruments to forge this single national market. More and more economic tools are being employed to ensure nationwide macroregulation and control and to harmonize relations between the open coastal areas and other parts of the country.

The Dual Character of Southern China

Southern China has a dual character in that it has both outward and inward orientation, the former based on its widely known economic complementarity with Hong Kong, Macao, and

Taiwan, and the latter on a crucial yet seldom-noticed complementarity with the vast hinterland. The great potentialities of the second complementarity have yet to be fully exploited simply because of insufficient development of the market economy as well as transportation and communications in the interior provinces.

Since 1949, China's industry—heavy industry in particular—has been mainly concentrated in the northeastern and island provinces. The same pattern is true for the distribution of natural resources and the technical workforce. In the wake of rapid economic progress in the coastal areas of Guangdong, Fujian, and other places, a set of highly significant policy measures has been adopted by the central government to strengthen these areas' economic links with the other parts of the country—a so-called inward-oriented expansion. These important measures include closer economic linkages between the coastal areas and the interior, encouragement of foreign investment in the hinterland, and expanded access to the southern open areas for inland enterprises.

Closer horizontal economic linkages between the coastal areas and the interior. Apart from sci-tech teamwork, horizontal linkages in materials exchange between Shenzhen, Guangdong, and Fujian, on the one hand, with other provinces or cities (including those in the hinterland) on the other, can be understood from table 6.1. The table demonstrates that the progress of horizontal economic association of the coastal areas is clearly greater than that of the cited inland areas. The total value of materials flowing out from and into the city of Shenzhen alone is higher not only than that for inland areas like Ningxia but also for the entire Fujian Province. This shows that China's SEZs and coastal open areas depend on both overseas and the interior for their capital, materials, and markets. China's open policy has a dual meaning: both outward and inward opening. The higher the degree of opening and the more advanced the market economy, the closer the economic linkages and exchanges with the overseas market and with other regions in China. To encourage horizontal linkages, the Chinese government has adopted a set of measures to eliminate arbitrary checkpoints and random charging of service fees.

Encouragement of foreign investment in the hinterland.
China's western, northern, and central regions constitute a vast untapped market. Foreign investors in coastal China often set

Table 6.1
Economic Linkages between China's Coastal and Inland Areas
(Unit: RMB 10,000 yuan)

	Outgoing materials	Incoming materials	Total
Coastal areas:			
Shenzhen Special Economic Zone	100,590	117,522	218,112
Guangdong Province	32,033	88,268	120,351
Fujian Province	31,162	30,675	61,833
Inland areas:			
Ningxia Autonomous Region	5,964	4,431	10,396
Qinghai Province	15,384	1,182	16,566
Xinjiang Autonomous Region	42,797	22,177	64,975

Source: China Almanac of Horizontal Economy Yearbook (Beijing), 1991.

their sights beyond these localities. Basing themselves there, they intend to extend their influence in all directions to penetrate markets in other provinces and cities. As the southern China market gradually becomes saturated, as is happening now, this tendency will grow more evident. Major Western transnationals are now increasing their investments in oil, coal, and infrastructure projects in China's hinterland—a new development worthy of attention.

Expanded access to the southern open areas for inland enterprises.   The Chinese central government demands that the open cities in southern China welcome the entry of enterprises from other parts of the country by providing them with favorable conditions. The SEZs in Guangdong and Fujian allow the establishment of agencies or representative offices from other provinces and cities and allow their products free entry to participate and compete in the SEZ markets. They also regard enterprises from other parts of the country as foreign-funded enterprises in terms of offering them similar treatment regarding land, factory sites, water and electric power supplies, and credit to facilitate their entry. All interior-linked enterprises operating in the SEZs pay an income tax on the spot at a preferential rate of 15 percent regardless of their ownership structure. Productive interior-linked enterprises operating in SEZs even receive preferential treatment in profit-sharing tax rates.

Interior-linked enterprises are expected to export their products, but partial domestic marketing is allowed for some enterprises in accordance with relevant regulations. Foreign-funded enterprises operating in the SEZs are also allowed to sell to China's domestic market those products not under state import restriction, providing they comply with the proportions stipulated in the relevant contracts and the volume of goods has been verified by the pertinent departments under the SEZ government.

In sum, it can be seen that it is absolutely impossible for China's SEZs or open areas—including those in southern China—to evolve into fully independent economic areas or groups, whether in the context of legislation or in actual economic activities.

The Center's Role in Coordinating the NET

In recent years, along with China's transition to a socialist market system, the central government has been increasingly employing economic means to coordinate its economic relations with coastal areas, including southern China. The State Council decision of December 15, 1993, to implement the Tax-Division Fiscal Management System stipulated that beginning January 1, 1994, tax revenues for the central and local governments were to be divided according to tax categories. The principles for division are the following: (1) taxes indispensable for the defense of national rights and for implementation of macroregulation and control are to be collected by the central government; (2) taxes directly related to economic development are to be shared by the central and local governments; and (3) taxes suitable for local collection remain held locally. The value-added tax is one of the major taxes for division, with the central government's share at 75 percent and the local government's at 25 percent. Generally speaking, since the implementation of the tax-sharing system, the portion going to the center has been enhanced to a certain extent.

A second economic instrument employed by the center encompasses financial means, including bank loans. Interest rates are now uniform across the country, and loan ceilings are subject to unified regulations to facilitate control over the scope of bank loans both nationwide and in specific localities. The notion of issuing a SEZ currency, once floated in the 1980s, has been dropped in favor of a national unified currency system.

Finally, the central government retains some investment funds to influence the growth rate of the entire nation or a particular region in order to promote economic restructuring. These funds are mostly invested in infrastructure projects or projects crucial to the expansion of the national economy. They may be used either in the coastal areas or in the interior at the discretion of the central government.

Lessons from the Southern China NET

The blossoming of NETs such as the southern China economic area has demonstrated to China and other parts of the world that a bright future awaits regional and subregional economic cooperation in Asia. NETs are exerting an ever-mounting influence on the economic development of the countries involved. They constitute a new form of regional and subregional economic cooperation best suited to the needs of Asia, where enormous differences exist in levels of socioeconomic development and the indigenous nature of socioeconomic systems. NETs make possible close economic cooperation among adjacent parts of neighboring countries having different levels of development and divergent social systems without any need to alter the socioeconomic system of the respective countries.

The southern China NET also symbolizes a window through which other parts of China can see the outside world, capture trends on the world markets, and explore ways to converge with the world markets and the global economy. Likewise, this NET window may help the outside world to better understand China's reform, opening, and policy trends. Its effect as a window, together with its widening influence in economic and technological fields, will surely multiply in the years ahead.

It is noteworthy that the effect of the southern China NET is not confined to the economic field only—it affects the mentality, work styles, and work procedures of the people involved. The question thus arises of how to converge with the international community in such fields. Before their hometowns were opened to the outside world, local leaders in places along the river and the border flocked to the open areas in southern China for on-the-spot investigation. Upon their return, they asked that the "consciousness of an open city take root in the mind of every citizen" and that "changes be made in ideas, work style, and work procedure of the people to satisfy the needs of opening." The multiplier effects of the NET in such fields will definitely be enhanced in the days to come.

7

The Politics of Economic Integration among Taiwan, Hong Kong, and Southern China

Robert S. Ross

The transformation of economic and social relations among Hong Kong, Taiwan, and mainland China during the past 15 years has been remarkable and far-reaching. Whereas political considerations once interfered with the development of natural economic relations, particularly for the People's Republic of China and Taiwan, today the barriers to such relations have been significantly reduced. The result has been a fundamental and, for the most part, positive change in the economic conditions of each of the three areas.

But economic relationships among independent units are never devoid of political implications. Insofar as economic development is a central foreign policy objective of such entities, they must consider the political and security implications of foreign economic ties. This is as true for China, Taiwan, and Hong Kong as for any other independent political entity—regardless of whether or not they possess the formal and legal attributes of sovereignty—and each must evaluate its own various bilateral economic relationships in the context of achieving its principal foreign policy objectives.

Over time, as economic relations grow, policymakers may find that the costs of pursuing political and security interests have increased, insofar as heightened political conflict can disrupt highly beneficial economic interests. The effect of closer economic relations will not be to eliminate conflicts of interest, but to make the cost of conflict higher. In such circumstances, policymakers will undoubtedly find themselves evaluating the economic implications of alternative foreign policies as they pursue traditional national interests, as well as the foreign policy implications of pursuing economic gains.

These considerations are as applicable to mainland China, Taiwan, and Hong Kong as they are to any other political entity in international relations. Thus, a central foreign policy issue for these areas is the implications of their growing involvement in the southern China economic region for the pursuit of their respective and often conflicting security interests.

The Political Ends of Economic Relations

For China, Taiwan, and, to a lesser extent, Hong Kong, economic development is one component of their more comprehensive national security policies. To the extent that their participation in the southern China economic region contributes to their respective modernization efforts, it also contributes to their security and foreign policy objectives.

The security implications of economic policy are particularly important for China, and Chinese leaders welcome the growing involvement of both Hong Kong and Taiwan in the Chinese economy for their significant contribution to Chinese modernization. Faced with the uncertainty of the post–cold war era and shifting relations among the great powers in East Asia, Chinese leaders are determined to develop "comprehensive national power"—they seek to develop the technological and scientific foundations for developing a world-class advanced economy as the basis for expanded international economic and military influence. Given China's relatively backward economy and its low level of science and technology compared with other regional powers, it has much catching up to do and needs all the help it can get. In this respect, Taiwan and Hong Kong play increasingly significant roles in China's effort to be a competitive strategic power in East Asia in the twenty-first century.

Taiwan also considers economic development a central component of its national security policy. At the most basic level, a strong and technologically advanced economy gives Taiwan the ability to develop its own defense and, ultimately, to deter the mainland from taking military action against it. Given the continued uncertainty about the reliability of its foreign sources of military equipment, Taiwan has been developing domestic military industries. The production of the Indigenous Defense Fighter is the most high-profile aspect of this policy. To continue this policy and develop more sophisticated and capable defense capabilities, Taiwan needs to maintain its current rate of economic growth. Economic growth also contributes to Taipei's effort to use economic diplomacy to expand its political presence in international affairs. Positive trade balances with the mainland and the high profits derived from production based on mainland manufacturing of Taiwan's export goods help Taipei maintain the foreign reserves it needs to develop a generous foreign aid program. Thus, Taiwan's ability to profit from the Chinese market and from inexpensive mainland labor can indirectly benefit its ability to resist mainland pressure.

Hong Kong, on the other hand, has no prospect of militarily providing for its security, and economic growth does not directly contribute to its defense. Nonetheless, to the extent that Hong Kong continues to develop its sophisticated economic infrastructure and to serve as an important entrepôt into the Chinese market, it will continue to attract investments from the major corporations of the advanced industrial countries. The presence of these corporations in Hong Kong serves as an economic trip wire; should China challenge the political and/or economic integrity of Hong Kong and, in so doing, harm the interests of the corporate giants of the advanced industrial countries, it will also place its political relationships with these important strategic powers at risk.

Thus, the development of the southern China economic region has served the security interests of each of the actors. Yet enhanced security does not obtain evenly among the three, and evidence suggests that Hong Kong and Taiwan may be undermining their long-term interests through greater economic interdependence with mainland China.

China and Taiwan: The Political Struggle over Independence

China's political interest in mainland-Taiwan trade is to reduce Taipei's ability to pursue its flexible foreign policy and, more important, to deter Taipei from declaring Taiwan an independent sovereign state. China has, for instance, granted Taiwan's commercial enterprises concessions that no other external enterprises receive, including less-severe import controls and favored tax treatment. In so doing, Beijing has sought to make Taiwan sufficiently dependent on the mainland economy that the potential costs of Chinese economic retaliation would deter any declaration of independence. It seeks the "Hong Kongization" of Taiwan.

Thus far, China can draw considerable satisfaction from attaining its objectives of cross-strait economic relations. As Sung Yun-wing points out in chapter 2 of this volume, Taiwan has developed a considerable stake in the stability of its investments and exports to the mainland, and their loss would adversely affect its economy. In contrast, Taiwan absorbs an insignificant portion of Chinese exports. It is important that Beijing has made these gains while avoiding significant political compromises; it continues to insist on the right to use force against Taiwan and its opposition to Taiwan's participation in international institutions dealing with any issue other than economics. Beijing recently conceded specific legal protection for Taiwanese investments on the mainland, reflecting China's willingness to reconsider its traditional stance that its domestic laws are sufficient to cover Taiwanese firms because Taiwan is a Chinese province. But it was no accident that the Chinese leadership made this decision only after Taiwan began to diversify its foreign investments away from the mainland and toward such Southeast Asian countries as Vietnam, Indonesia, and the Philippines. When Chinese leaders faced competitors for Taiwan's capital and thus a challenge to the political objectives of their Taiwan economic policy, they compromised.

Taiwan's leadership and people also have political objectives that they pursue through economic relations with the mainland. But whereas the mainland hopes to use cross-strait economic ties to constrain Taiwan's independence in foreign policy, Taipei tries to use its mainland economic policy to expand its ability to challenge China's insistence that Taiwan adhere to a one-China foreign policy. Despite the civil war rhetoric of the Kuomintang leadership, it is difficult to detect any interest on the part of any Taiwan political party or political leader in reunifying with China. On the other hand, Taiwan's interest in de facto and de jure independence are manifest: both would contribute to its security from mainland forces, promote the government's long-term stability, and afford the people on Taiwan the respect from the international system they feel they deserve.

Thus, while recognizing the danger of developing economic dependency on the Chinese market, Taipei tries to hold hostage China's growing stake in stable economic relations and the prospect of improved political relations to limit Beijing's ability to pressure it into abandoning its flexible foreign policy. The cross-strait dialogue and the Koo-Wang talks have also served this purpose for Taiwan.[1] In turn, Taipei seeks to use its flexible foreign policy both to offset its dependence on the Chinese economy and to enhance its security by improving its international political status through expanded participation in international multilateral institutions and a greater political presence in countries through the use of foreign aid. For Taipei, mainland-Taiwan economic relations are ultimately aimed at helping it to resist the pressure for political reunification and compliance with Beijing's demand that Taiwan pursue a strict one-China policy.

Thus far, however, the mainland portion of Taiwan's own "independent foreign policy" is developing faster than its effort to establish an expanded political role in world affairs. Since it relaxed restrictions on trade with the mainland, China's strategic position in northeast Asia has improved so that the incentive for Taiwan's neighbors to risk Chinese opposition to improve ties with Taiwan has declined considerably. This is the case for Japan, South Korea, and Russia; as for the United States, the instability in U.S.-China relations tends to deter Washington from risking further conflict with Beijing by challenging Chinese interests in Taiwan. Moreover, the spectacular growth of the Chinese economy in recent years has increased the interest of all of the advanced industrial economies in consolidating ties with Beijing. Thus, in the mainland-Taiwan competition for international support, Taiwan's position has been deteriorating.

This is exemplified by several events in recent years. Taiwan lost its diplomatic recognition from South Korea; its president was asked by the United States not to attend the Asia-Pacific Economic Cooperation (APEC) summit in Seattle; it has aroused almost no support for its effort to participate in the United Nations (UN); and it is unlikely that it will be able to join any UN-affiliated economic institutions. Its relations with European countries have fared no better. France, succumbing to Chinese economic pressure, agreed to curtail arms sales to Taipei, and Germany has clearly decided that economic relations with China are a high priority. To varying degrees, all of the European countries are placing a similar emphasis on economic relations with China, and Taiwan's position in these countries' foreign policies has correspondingly suffered. The exceptions to this trend prove the rule. Where China is relatively less important, Taiwan has been more successful. President Lee Teng-hui's "vacation diplomacy" was successful in Southeast Asia because of all the countries of East Asia, those have the least extensive economic ties with China and are less susceptible to Chinese political influence. (Yet even they have agreed to exclude Taiwan from the Regional Forum of the Association of Southeast Asian Nations.) It is likely that Taiwan will be admitted into the World Trade Organization (WTO). Insofar as mainland China's entry into the WTO will, in the short run, be disadvantageous for the advanced industrial countries, they have been in no hurry to admit Beijing, so Beijing has been compelled to accommodate itself to U.S. interests regarding Taiwan membership.

It seems that the political implications of Taiwan's participation in the development of the southern China economic region have thus far been detrimental to Taiwan's foreign policy goals. Its dependency on the mainland economy has been growing, and it has been only minimally successful in offsetting this dependency with an enhanced political role in world affairs. Should present economic and political trends continue, the effect of cross-strait economic relations will be to reduce Taiwan's ability to deter Beijing from retaliating against its effort to maximize its political independence and, ultimately, its long-term autonomy. Thus, Taipei must consider whether the political costs of participation in the southern China economic zone have begun to exceed the economic benefits.

In these circumstances, it is not surprising that Taiwan has begun to develop its "southward" policy, trying to diversify its direct overseas investments and regain some of the economic independence it lost after the expansion of cross-strait economic relations. Taipei will also maintain restrictions on investments on the mainland to minimize its dependence on China for sensitive products and to maintain indigenous production of goods that it can still produce at internationally competitive costs. Similarly, Taipei will be reluctant to legitimate "direct" trade with the mainland without prior significant achievements in its flexible foreign policy and some greater diversification of its economic relationships.

China and Hong Kong: The Struggle over Democracy

Security and political issues are also entwined in Hong Kong-mainland relations. Although Hong Kong's international political future has been resolved, the nature of its internal political system remains uncertain. In the years leading up to 1997, many people in Hong Kong have wanted to establish democratic institutions to maximize their post-1997 autonomy from Beijing. China, on the other hand, has the opposite objective for Hong Kong. It wants to maximize its authority over Hong Kong both now and after 1997. As in mainland-Taiwan relations, Hong Kong and Beijing want to use economic relations to achieve their respective, conflicting objectives.

Hong Kong has clearly become a part of the Chinese economy, and its economic future is now intimately tied to policies

made in Beijing. As Sung Yun-wing notes in chapter 2, Hong
Kong's manufacturing industry and a significant portion of its
investment capital have moved to southern China. Unlike Taiwan, however, Hong Kong does not possess a military force nor
even the slightest semblance of international political legitimacy
as an independent state. That Hong Kong is part of China and
will return to Chinese rule in 1997 is undisputed in international
politics, giving the mainland the uncontested ability to determine Hong Kong's political and economic fate.

In important respects, however, China's leverage over Hong
Kong is not new. China's military superiority has existed since
1949, and its control over food and water supplies to Hong Kong
have long cautioned Hong Kong authorities against testing Chinese tolerance. Nonetheless, the economic integration between
Hong Kong and southern China has now entwined the daily
lives of the Hong Kong people with the unpredictable politics of
the Chinese leadership in Beijing. Thus, the sensitivity of the
people of Hong Kong to Chinese interests has deepened with the
integration of Hong Kong into the southern China economic
region.

But the more fundamental change in Hong Kong-mainland
relations has been the development of Chinese economic interests in the evolution of Hong Kong's internal affairs. The economic benefits that China derives from Hong Kong now
contribute significantly to Chinese economic development and
to the living standards in southern China. Hong Kong has
always been vulnerable to developments in China; now China is
sensitive to developments in Hong Kong. In contrast to the past,
when there was only Hong Kong's economic vulnerability to
Chinese power, and in contrast to contemporary mainland-
Taiwan relations, there has developed in recent years a significant degree of mutual economic vulnerability between Hong
Kong and the mainland. Moreover, Beijing's Hong Kong policy
has symbolic importance for mainland-Taiwan relations; the
Chinese leadership has a considerable interest in proving its
ability to accommodate different forms of government on
Chinese territory.

Hong Kong's important role in mainland economic development and foreign policy and its focus on domestic change give it
greater ability than Taiwan to achieve its objectives. In contrast
with Taiwan's interest in independence, which requires it to alter
the international status quo and which would compel other
states to choose between Taipei and Beijing, Hong Kong's effort

to change its domestic system entails unilateral efforts, which have far less impact on its relationships with other actors. For this reason, Hong Kong would seem to have greater maneuverability than Taiwan in promoting its interests vis-à-vis the mainland.

Nonetheless, despite Beijing's significant interest in stable economic relations with Hong Kong, Chinese leaders clearly have a greater interest in preventing the development of an autonomous Hong Kong government independent of Beijing's will. An autonomous Hong Kong protecting civil liberties and challenging Beijing's authority would have a powerful and threatening demonstration effect, stimulating Chinese throughout the mainland to challenge Beijing's authority and to seek democratic institutions for the entire country. In addition, a democratic and autonomous Hong Kong government might actively encourage democracy activists in China, and Hong Kong could become a sanctuary for Chinese activists and a hospitable environment for Chinese "revolutionaries." Although this might seem a rather far-fetched scenario, the treaty ports played such a role in the early twentieth century. Given such concerns, it is not surprising that Beijing would like to establish even greater authority over Hong Kong policy-making in the pre-1997 years.

Thus, whereas there may be a semblance of mutual economic dependency between the mainland and Hong Kong, the possibility exists that the Chinese leadership will value a compliant and submissive Hong Kong government more than the economic benefits it derives from the Hong Kong economy. And given the sensitivity in Chinese elite politics to the issue of party control over Hong Kong, individual Chinese leaders are apt to sacrifice China's economic interests in stable relations with Hong Kong in order to survive their own succession politics. The delay of the post–Deng Xiaoping succession into the mid-1990s suggests that China's economic interests may not be the primary concern of Chinese leaders as the date of Hong Kong's return to China approaches.

This is not to say that succession-minded Chinese leaders will quickly institute formal Chinese financial or political control over Hong Kong's economic and political systems (although they might), but that heavy-handed Chinese measures aimed at reasserting the symbols of Chinese sovereignty over Hong Kong and at deterring the development of a democracy movement in Hong Kong could seriously shake the confidence of the Hong

Kong business community, lead to human and capital flight, and undermine the strengths of the Hong Kong economy. This would have a catastrophic effect on the interests of the people of Hong Kong. The unfortunate coincidence of the Chinese political succession with the return of Hong Kong to China in 1997, the serious challenge posed by an autonomous and democratic Hong Kong to the Chinese leadership, and the vulnerability of Hong Kong to Chinese policy combine to undermine Hong Kong's ability to offer its economy as hostage in order to develop democratic institutions.

Nonetheless, many people in Hong Kong are not content to passively accept the status quo, for they too have important security objectives. The violent repression of the Chinese democracy movement in June 1989, the continued inability of China to develop a predictable legal system free from arbitrary and capricious decision making, the ongoing suppression in China of the most basic civil liberties, and the extreme instability in Chinese politics all underscore to the people of Hong Kong just how vulnerable their political and economic system will be after 1997, despite Chinese statements to the contrary. These security concerns have compelled them to try to maximize the prospects for maintaining their personal security after 1997 by transferring political power to the voters from unelected leaders who can simply "hand over power" to the Chinese Communist Party. Sure that the possibility of developing such institutions will be stronger before 1997 than after, the people of Hong Kong are in a hurry to change their political system.

Thus China and Hong Kong face a stalemate, each dissatisfied with the status quo but each reluctant to challenge it—China for fear that it will lose the economic benefits of a stable Hong Kong, Hong Kong for fear of inciting a Chinese reaction destructive its ability to maintain minimal economic and political flexibility. The result is the familiar testing and probing, advance and retreat policies that have come to characterize relations between the Hong Kong government and Beijing. Each side is uncertain what will elicit an excessive response from its counterpart, so each is willing to risk challenging the status quo only at the margins. Thus the basic parameters of current Hong Kong–mainland relations and of the Hong Kong political system will probably remain intact through 1997.

Conclusion

The development of the southern China economic region has been a positive development for the economies of all three of its components. The people of China, Hong Kong, and Taiwan are all growing richer from the expansion of subregional economic relations. This is a major accomplishment.

But the impressive economic integration among these three economies has not reduced the importance to each of the search for greater security and of the resulting political conflicts between them. On the contrary, as economic integration has developed, security concerns and political conflicts have deepened. Demands for independence on Taiwan and China's corresponding concern have grown as mainland-Taiwan economic ties have expanded. Meanwhile, China's blossoming economic power and improved global position have undermined Taipei's ability to pursue its flexible foreign policy. Similarly, the absorption of the Hong Kong economy into the southern China economy has coincided with growing demands for democracy in Hong Kong and with increased Chinese concern about the implications of a democratic Hong Kong for the stability of the Chinese Communist Party. It has also coincided with increased instability in elite Chinese politics, underscoring to the people of Hong Kong their vulnerability to arbitrary Chinese power and the importance of consolidating their decision-making autonomy before 1997.

Economic integration has not reduced political conflict. The most positive statement that can be made about the implications of economic integration for the politics of independence and democracy is that it has increased the potential costs of escalated political conflict, which may deter all sides from adopting belligerent policies and motivate a search for mutually satisfactory negotiated solutions. Yet it is also possible that the present integration of the three economies may simply make the future tragedies of conflict over intractable political issues all the more painful to endure.

Notes

1. For more detail on the Koo-Wang talks, see note 20 in chapter 1.